The Station of Man in the Universe

THE
STATION of MAN
IN THE
UNIVERSE

EBENEZER SIBLY
ON THE
SPIRIT WORLD and MAGIC

WITH A GENERAL INTRODUCTION BY

JOHN MADZIARCZYK, ED.

TOPAZ HOUSE PUBLICATIONS

SEATTLE, WA MMXIV.

Copyright Topaz House Publications, 2014
Introduction copyright John Madziarczyk
No parts of this book may be reproduced by any means except for brief quotations.
ISBN: 978-0-9906682-0-6

www.topazbooks.pub

I would like to thank the publishers, writers, and academics dedicated to bringing forth a new understanding of old esotericism, without whom this book would not be possible, as well as Eric Purdue for the translations of the Latin and insights into their sources.

—J.M.

Contents

Introduction	9
To the Young Student in Astrology	49
Poetical Invocation to Urania	51
Part the First	53
A Summary View of the Works of Creation, in the Construction of Nature	69
Part the Fourth.	99

Introduction:

Ebenezer Sibly was a magician, astrologer, and physician who wanted to be taken seriously by the scientific establishment. Known for casting the horoscope of the United States, he was perhaps the last great representative of the British magical worldview of the 17th century best exemplified by astrologer William Lilly, herbalist Nicholas Culpepper, and the translator Robert Turner, among others. To the list can be added Thomas Vaughan and Elias Ashmole. Living at the end of the 18th century Sibly fought valiantly to reconcile astrology, natural magic, and herbalism with both science and mainstream medicine, and to justify it to an increasingly skeptical public. To help in the fight he enlisted Swedenborg and Mesmer. It was a losing battle. Sibly's point of view would peter out after his death, until the occultism of the 17th century ceased to be a living tradition.

The occult world of 17th century Great Britain was a unique blend of science and esotericism that was formed before the final split between the two occurred. Francis Yates, in "The Rosicrucian Enlightenment", charts the course of these alchemists, scientists, and mystics of the time, who tried to formulate a "Rosicrucian" vision of science that preserved Renaissance occult notions while incorporating the new discoveries. Though specifically referring to a subset of people, the ethos behind the "Rosicrucian Enlightenment" was broadly shared by esotericists, albeit in a fairly unorganized way. Although they failed to create a lasting paradigm, they inadvertently founded some of the primary institutions that helped move science forward, such as the Royal Society and the British Museum. It was also a time of intensive work with grimoires and magic. Books such as Agrippa's "Three Books of Occult Philosophy" and "Fourth Book" were translated into English, and grimoires flourished in manuscript form, including those still used today. Although Sibly never described himself as a "Rosicrucian", their belief in the compatibility of science and the occult, as well as more covert occult work, continued in his thought.

After Sibly, the split between science and the occult became permanent. While the occultists who were immediately influenced by him continued the synthesis, they didn't try to present it to the greater public, and as time went on, occult thought drew into itself. Although some currents present in Sibly's time continued, such as Animal Magnetism and the thought of Swedenborg, occult thought as a whole became increasingly hostile to science. The occult writers of the middle to late 19th century preferred the strange and unusual, history from the dawn of time, to writers of a few centuries before. As they became a purely counter-cultural movement, their influence dwindled.

It wouldn't be until the rise of the Theosophical Society several decades later that occultism would start to become a renewed force in society as a whole. The TS, however, approached the subject from the opposite shore from Sibly. For Sibly, magic was still alive, and science was the challenger. Magic was the elder statesman, if you will. The Theosophical Society, on the other hand, coming from a wholly modern worldview, attempted to justify magic through science. Much of the first volume of Blavatsky's "Isis Unveiled" is dedicated to proving that the latest findings of science are really rediscoveries of occult principles. Still, the TS represented a continuity of the occult tradition. It's initial sources came from Spiritualism, inspired in part by Swedenborg, and psychical research, inspired in part by Anton Mesmer. While the TS was concerned with all aspects of occultism, it nevertheless kept its distance from practical magic. Magic would have to wait until the turn of the 20th century, and publications by individuals associated with the Golden Dawn, to emerge back into the popular consciousness.

Sibly represents a link in the chain in the history of British ceremonial magic that connects the Golden Dawn to the time of Lilly. Along the way, that chain passes through the Societas Rosicrucia In Anglia, the crystal scrying of self declared Rosicrucian Frederick Hockley, and the world of occult book selling and publishing, which drew heavily on Sibly's manuscripts.

The main text reproduced here is an anachronism in Sibly's printed work. It is the fourth part of "A New and Complete Illustration of the Celestial Science of Astrology", and deals explicitly with magic, as well as with the spirit world in general. At over a thousand pages, the overwhelming majority of "A New Complete Illustration" is concerned with astrology, but Sibly chose to make the last, and smallest, part a survey of the rest of occultism. Although ostensibly framed in the language of moral concern, Sibly cites and describes magical practices to the point where the work resembles an introduction to both the magical world and occult practices in general rather than a polemic against them. The other texts reproduced here directly shed light on Sibly's view of the greater universe, even though they do not explicitly deal with magic. Together, they function as a window into the worldview of a magical practitioner from a time where commonly known attestations are slim to none, with a few notable exceptions, including the grimoires themselves. The works here deal with topics as diverse as how the spiritual universe is structured, what happens after people die, and how to call up the dead.

Sibly's Life

Sibly was born in 1751 and died in 1799, before the age of fifty. Paul Kléber Monod states that his father was a carpenter[i]. He had two sisters, of whom not much is known, and one brother, who became a notable Swedenborgian minister. He grew up in Bristol, an industrial town in England south of Wales, and moved from there to Portsmouth, and back, before leaving for London around 1788[ii].

It's not known if Sibly was initially taught medicine or was self taught. However, Paul Monod[iii] points to a tribute that Sibly wrote in memory of "The Quaker doctor John Till Adams" of Bristol as an indication that Adams was a mentor. Later in life Sibly attempted to professionalize himself by getting an M.D. from King's College in Aberdeen, Scotland. While Debus [iv] remarks that he possibly got the degree without ever traveling to Scotland, it still reflects a desire to be taken more seriously by the mainstream of British medicine.

His first work was "A New Complete Illustration of the Celestial Science of Astrology", issued in four parts over the course of four years, starting in 1784 and ending in 1788 [v]. According to Davies[vi], Sibly moved to London from Bristol the year the last part was issued. Davies suggests[vii] that the work as a whole served as an advertisement of his familiarity with occult texts to the general public, which also presumably included

i   Monod, 274
ii Davies, "Grimoires",134
iii Monod, 275
iv Debus, 260
v   ibid., 260
vi Davies, "Grimoires", 134
vii ibid., 135

the London esoteric literati. In finding his way into the London occult world, his brother Manoah may have helped.

Although Manoah was the younger brother, he preceded Ebenezer in London, and set up a publishing firm[i] that reprinted astrological classics. A Swedenborgian minister at the time Ebenezer moved to the capitol, he presumably had contacts within that community. Swedenborg burst onto the scene in 1758 with his book "Heaven and Hell", that contained accounts of tours given to him of both of them, and of other regions, given by the angels themselves. "Heaven and Hell" was originally written in Latin, and was only fully translated into English in 1778 by Thomas Hartley. The thought of Swedenborg gave new life to the nascent occult world, and became one of the two ascendant forces challenging the increasingly reductionist philosophy of the day, the other being the Animal Magnetism of Anton Mesmer. Mesmer moved to Paris and started promoting his practices in 1778. The doctrine of Swedenborg drew those with occult interests, and the Swedenborgian community in London was divided between those who had occult interests and those who were purely Christian[ii]. Manoah's later sermons indicated little interest in the broader occult world, and he left publishing and became a career civil servant with the Bank of England[iii].

Ebenezer Sibly did well in London. His "A New Complete Illustration of the Celestial Science of Astrology" was followed in 1789 by a revised edition of Nicholas Culpeper's "The English Physician". After getting his M.D. in 1792, Sibly published "The Medical Mirror", a treatise on women's health. "A Key to Physic and the Occult Sciences", followed in 1794, and attempted to reconcile medicine, and natural history, with occultism as a whole. Finally, beginning in 1796 Sibly started a series of publications titled "Magazine of natural history comprehending the whole science of animals, plants, and minerals. ", also known as the "Natural History", which continued the synthesis.

Both Davies and Monod cast Sibly as either one of the[iv], or the most influential occult writers of his time[v], with Davies writing that Sibly was "one of the most influential occultists in modern British history"[vi]. Debus

---

i   Monod, 276
ii   Godwin, 102
iii   ibid, 106
iv   Monod, 274
v   Davies, "Grimoires", 134
vi   ibid.

has traced the publication history of all his works[i]. By 1821 "A New Illustration" was in its twelfth edition. The last edition Debus saw came out in 1826. Sibly's edition of "The English Physician" "reached a thirteenth edition by 1821"[ii]. His more philosophical "Key to Physic" reached a fifth edition in 1814[iii], and his book on women's health, "The Medical Mirror" reached its sixth edition by 1814[iv]. Manod reports that Sibly also opened up his own publishing firm, the British Directory Office[v], and at least the first printing of Sibly's expanded edition of Nicholas Culpeper's "English Physician" was published there. Debus also states that some of the later printings of Culpeper were versions of Sibly's edition that did not include his name[vi], and indeed some of the recent reprints floating around the internet are actually unacknowledged copies of Sibly's work.

What may have contributed to the popularity of Sibly's writings was that even though they contained occult material they were aimed at people who, though literate, didn't have much of a background in higher education. In the era Sibly lived occult learning was democratized through authors tapping into the emerging market of people who worked in trades or professions, were literate, and were either self educated, or had a minimal education. This completed a trend that began in the 17th century, when Lilly, Culpeper, and others decided to write their works in English instead of Latin, and when many texts were translated from Latin into English. As Monod says about a guide to astrology that came out a year after the first installment of "A New Illustration", its audience were people who were "More familiar with the Bible than with Newton"[vii]. The first glimmerings in these last years of the 19th century of the cultural trend that would give rise to the English Romantic and Gothic movements in literature, which Monod[viii] and Davies[ix] cite, may also have contributed to the popularity of Sibly's work.

---

i   Debus, 261-262
ii ibid.
iii ibid.
iv ibid.
v   Monod, 276
vi Debus, 261
vii Monod, 274
viii ibid., 228
ix Davies, "Grimoires", 134

The Occult World of Sibly

As for the occult world that Sibly himself lived in, there really wasn't a public one, at least initially. Sibly's works came at the end of a long drought in interest in the occult, and through their popularity contributed to the end of the draught and the formation of a new occult scene in Great Britain. There were, of course, other occultists at the time, but their publications were scarce. "The Conjuror's Magazine", later titled "The Astrologer's Magazine and Philosophical Miscellany", stands out as an exception. However, even "The Conjuror's Magazine" only started publication in 1791, seven years after the first installment of "A New Illustration" was issued. For our purposes, Sibly's circle can best be seen as these occultists, a small number of others he knew, plus those he influenced through his printed and manuscript works. "The Conjuror", and it's anonymous authors, though hostile to Sibly, serve as a documentary bridge between Sibly and these later individuals. Part of the gap in evidence between Sibly and his successors reflects bigger trends in British occult history. There was little public activity between the mid 1790s and the 1820s, and this was caused by the politics of the day. These were the French Revolution and the wars between Great Britain and France.

According to both Monod and Godwin while the 1780s saw a certain increase in openness to esoteric subjects, if not an increase in publications, this slammed shut with France's declaration of war against England in 1793[i,ii]. England stayed at war against revolutionary France until 1802, and took up the leading role in a series of coalitions against Napoleon from 1803-1815. Monod recounts in detail how the start of war between France and England lead to a wave of suspicion against those who did not conform, and lead to an increased pressure to fit in[iii]. Occult groups and practices came in for increased scrutiny[iv], and the association of Mesmer with France didn't likely help.

Even before the war, there were acts of violence committed against those who publicly spoke out in favor of the French Revolution. In the "Priestly Riots" that took place in Birmingham, Joseph Priestly, a partisan of the radical Enlightenment and a reformist theologian, had his house looted and burned to the ground in 1791 as the culmination of a mass riot against a group of his friends who had organized a public banquet to

i   Monod, 227
ii Godwin, 115
iii Monod, 300
iv ibid., 301

celebrate Bastille Day, the traditional start of the Revolution[i]. The riots were also aimed against Dissenters, who were members of Protestant groups that were not part of the Church of England, such as Methodists and Baptists. Secret societies were subject to distrust, and were suspected of being bases for fifth columns of infiltrators. This dramatically cut the amount of occult publications that were issued, and even "The Astrologers' Magazine" ceased publication in 1794.

The situation was worsened by the publication in English of the Abbe Barruel's "Memoirs Illustrating the History of Jacobinism". This multi-volume work, appearing in French in 1797-1798 and in English in 1799, aimed to pin the origins of the radical French Revolution on the Illuminati, Freemasonry , and occult groups in general. Although Barruel's work is most famous for its treatment of the Illuminati, the other volumes also listed virtually every major Masonic and esoteric group in France as potential fronts for the conspiracy, including ones that were very Christian. Coming in the middle of what turned out to be over twenty years of war with France, this fanned the flames of reaction against occultists even more[ii]. Groups in Great Britain who were associated with those named by Barruel endeavored to prove their loyalty by purging themselves of any elements perceived to be suspect, which included most of those that were unorthodox, occult, and politically radical[iii]. Monod[iv] and Godwin[v] point out that between 1793 and 1815 the only major new occult publication was "The Magus" by Barrett, appearing in 1801. Sibly's "Key to Physic and the Occult Sciences" was published in 1794.

Monod illustrates the mood by pointing to John Parkins' advertisement titled "A Cabinet of Wealth", published in 1812[vi]. Parkins, who we'll see later, was a cunning man, a student of Barrett, a friend of Sibly, and an associate of bookseller John Denley. "A Cabinet of Wealth" was a large brochure that advertized his services, as well as writings that he only sold as manuscripts. After the preface, Parkins makes sure to set "GOD SAVE THE KING, AND DEFEND THIS NATION!" in large type , and at the start of the introduction lists himself as "Dr. Parkins, of Little Gonerby,

---

i   Monod, 304
ii ibid., 300
iii ibid., 301
iv ibid., 300
v   Godwin 116
vi Monod, 301

Near Grantham, Lincolnshire, Who is a Servant of God, and a most dutiful subject to the best of Monarchs;"

As for the return of occult publishing, Monod[i] cites a book on "apparitions and spirits" put out by Lackington publishers and booksellers in 1814 as one of the first examples. The publisher was careful to say that they believed that the subject matter was superstitious. Lackington's subsequent publication of "The Lives of the Alchemystical Philosophers" in 1815 is cited by Monod as another faint indicator of the return of the acceptability of publishing occult books[ii]. When occult publishing did return, a great deal of it was catalyzed by the circle around bookseller John Denley, who came into possession of many of Sibly's manuscripts after his death. Denley himself contributed to it by publishing "A Philosophical Merlin", a guide to Geomancy, by Robert Cross Smith in 1822. Smith, an astrologer and occultist, would in turn have a major role in occult publishing himself as the man behind several magazines and at least five books.

After occult publishing fully returned to Great Britain, it followed a much different path than before. It featured much less of an awareness of Enlightenment philosophy and science, and little if any political content. The circle around Denley continued Sibly's general worldview in the post-Napoleon world, but in a changed fashion, and eventually their disciplined approach, which continued the worldview of the 17th century, gave way to impulses to fantasy and sensationalism. While respectfully treating recent developments in the occult such as animal magnetism and spiritism, the mid 19th century saw the rise of occult publishing that traded on interest in the supernatural to sell outright fraudulent material, presented in a suitably mysterious package.

"The Conjuror's Magazine", though, provides a good example of the road not taken, of a type of occultism that emerged in the late 18th century, that originated from the same point of view as that of Sibly, but took it in a different direction, one that was essentially quashed by the conflict between England and France that started in 1793.

The Conjuror's Magazine.

The magazine had two incarnations. First, between 1791 and 1793 it was "The Conjuror's Magazine", devoting itself to occultism in general, astrology, tales of the supernatural, ghosts, and stage magic. In 1793 it

---

[i] Monod, 300
[ii] ibid., 301

reinvented itself as "The Astrologers' Magazine and Philosophical Miscellany", focussed more on astrology, and ran until 1794. The magazine's writers and publishers were anonymous, with their names replaced by initials. Marsha Schuchard, however[i], has named the editor and likely publisher as Henry Lemoine, a French Huegenot printer and bookseller living in London. Though Godwin reports in "The Theosophical Enlightenment"[ii] that "The Conjuror" had a different philosophical view than Sibly, and denounced him as an inept plagiarizer, the differences, although significant, appear to have been much more minor than indicated. The authors were certainly critical of "A New and Complete Illustration". I have not seen copies of "The Astrologers' Magazine", but I have seen all the issues of "The Conjuror", which were re-issued in a two volume set.

What "The Conjuror" did was blend the 17th century view of occultism with the more cutting edge Enlightenment philosophy of its time. It took an interest both in low and high magic but combined these beliefs with an editorial view that saw both as based on materialism , where the "Materia" was thought to be itself spiritual. The magazine itself was far from dogmatic about its positions. They rarely denounced any spiritual practice as superstition, and in fact reproduced manuals on just about anything, from divination by moles all the way up to Raymond Llull's thought. One thing the magazine is notable for is that it contained much less religious content in their articles than other publications of the time.

A typical issue would feature an astrological chart with interpretation, essays devoted to philosophical analyses of occultism, extracts of classic texts like the Petit Albert or the Arbatel, and manuals on divination such as Palmistry, followed by recent accounts of supernatural phenomenon, instructions on card tricks, logic problems, stage magic, book reviews, rounded out by correspondence. As for their treatment of Sibly, the negative review of "A New Complete Illustration" appears in the April 1792 issue of "The Conjuror". It reads:

"Mercutio requires our opinion of the 'Illustration of Astrology.' To this we answer, that, we only esteem it a quack performance, very unequally executed, by a head incompetent to the task of either composing or compiling; for in it we discover all the blunders of old John Gadbury,

---

    i   Schuchard, "Rediscovering William 'The Hurricane' Gilbert"
    ii Godwin, 116

introduced without correction or distinction, in the very language of Bedlam."

To add insult to injury, the mention follows after a list of astrological books new students should look to.

There may have been a tinge of class resentment behind these condemnations. Sibly was largely self educated, and even though he cited scientists and physicians from his day he wasn't really concerned with current philosophy as a whole. He didn't have an elite education and was not connected to the literati of his time. In this, he was reflective of a great many people who had begun to make their way into the lower middle and middle middle class in the late 18th century. In his writings Sibly appears to have been mostly concerned with what was going on that intersected with his own concerns, and he tended to ignore the rest. Tellingly, in the third essay reproduced here, one of the main arguments for the existence of God is a series of paragraphs that come from a work written in 1705. While his indifference may have made Sibly more popular with his audience, who likely didn't know about the latest discussions in philosophy, it wouldn't have endeared him to those who did.

The editors and contributors to "The Conjuror" were much more keyed into current intellectual thought, at the least through the editorship of Lemoine, who was likely responsible for the translation and inclusion of works by alchemist Pierre-Jean Fabre in the magazine under the name of "Peter John Faber". Even though they printed just about anything, "The Conjuror" was notable for featuring a greater amount of material from the high tradition of ceremonial magic than later, similar, publications such as "The Straggling Astrologer". Indeed, the editors of "The Conjuror" may have been too cutting edge for their own good.

Monod cites a very interesting passage[i] in the September 1793 issue of "The Astrologers' Magazine", printed after France had declared war on England, where a writer calling himself "Astrologus" responds to a letter asking about the astrological view of military operations on the continent by saying, in part:

"Monarchy, therefore, being abolished in France, the querent is anxious, as many other friends to the peace and happiness of mankind appear to be, that the French Republic may be indivisible, incorruptible, and immortal, and that by proving a salutary lesson to tyrants in every clime, and of every description, that revolution may preclude the necessity of others"

---

i   Monod 303-304

Considering that the Huegenots, of which editor Henry Lemoine was one, were a persecuted minority in Catholic France, this perspective is understandable, but in the context of the times it was potentially treasonous, to say the least. "The Astrologers' Magazine" ceased publication in 1794, although the exact reasons for this are unknown. After the French Revolution and the Napoleonic wars, political radicalism and occultism wouldn't combine again in Great Britain until the rise of the Theosophical Society.

The Post-Sibly circle

Sibly died in 1799. His manuscript collection was bought from his cousin by the book seller and publisher Lackington. Subsequently, many of the manuscripts were bought by the bookseller John Denley. Denley's shop was one of the best occult bookstores in England at the time[i], and he supplemented his income by making copies of magical manuscripts for customers, including those from Sibly's collection. Denley operated his shop for a very long time, long enough to wait out the Napoleonic wars and to help to foster a renewal of occult publishing in Great Britain.

Francis Barrett of "The Magus" and his student John Parkins were two early Denley associates who in the case of Parkins, either definitely knew Sibly[ii], or in the case of Barrett, potentially knew him,[iii] or at the least made use of his works. Francis King makes a good circumstantial case in his book "The Flying Sorcerer", that Barrett and Sibly knew each other based on living in close proximity. Barrett, who published "The Magus" in 1801, was certainly in the area at the time, and his student Parkins definitely knew the man before his death. Also, Barrett was a crystal scryer, and passed this onto Parkins[iv], and while there may have been many sources for this, Sibly may have been one. Reasons for a possible connection between Sibly and Barrett via crystal gazing will be gone over in the section on Sibly's writings themselves.

According to Frederick Hockley[v], Barrett made great use of the manuscripts that Denley had acquired after Sibly's death in compiling "The Magus", and Owen Davies reconstructs the story in "Cunning Folk", adding that Denley later got his revenge by buying the plates,

i Davies, "Grimoires", 134
ii King, 40
iii ibid.
iv ibid., 39
v Hamil, 31

engravings, and woodblocks for "The Magus" after the book went out of print. Denley chose not to reprint the book, and his ownership of all the equipment prevented anyone else from reprinting it[i]. This made it an increasingly scarce work in the 19th century[ii] and, ironically, made it a book whose reputation exceeded its practical use.

John Parkins, a student of Barrett who knew Sibly, is an interesting subject in and of himself. He's said by Davies to be one of the first Cunning Men to make use of print advertisements to offer his services[iii]. Specifically, he advertised various talismans he could make to help with various issues as well as books that he wrote that were only available as manuscripts, and from him directly. Davies in "Cunning Folk" relates that Parkins provoked a remarkable pamphlet titled "Ecce Homo! Critical remarks on the infamous publications of J. Parkins"[iv], likely written by a disgruntled client. However, although entertaining, recounting that story would take us too far afield.

Parkins' documentation as a student of Barrett comes from Francis King's short but essential marshaling of primary sources available about Barrett, "The Flying Sorcerer", where he documents that Parkins copied an unpublished essay by Barrett on crystal gazing into his commonplace book shortly after the essay was written[v]. King's book also provides a direct source connecting Parkins to Sibly. He cites a statement by Parkins in his "Book of Miracles", first published in 1817, that Sibly had Saturn and Mars in his seventh house, and that "the consequence was this; he had two or three wives, but could not live with any of them", before stating that he had either stayed with Sibly in London or visited him frequently in 1796, during which time Sibly "was then living in a state of separation from his wife, whom I never saw all the while I was in town"[vi]. Parkins was active in the decade during the Napoleonic wars, but covertly. The rest of the Denley associates of note started their association with him in the 1820s.

---

i   Davies, "Cunning Folk", 142-143
ii ibid. 143,
iii ibid., 116-117
iv ibid., 51-52
v   King, 39
vi King, 40

Robert Cross Smith

The most literarily prolific member of Denley's circle in the 1820s was Robert Cross Smith, the first "Raphael" of the eponymous series of Ephemerides. Smith also produced the magazines "The Straggling Astrologer", "Urania " and the "Prophetic Almanack". The first two contained a mixture of astrology, fiction, and magical material drawn from manuscripts belonging to Denley and others, including those that belonged to Sibly. The contents of these magazines appear to have resembled the "The Conjuror's Magazine". Although the magazines themselves are obscure, what they contained can be inferred through Smith's later publications, "The Astrologer in the Nineteenth Century" and "The Familiar Astrologer", both of which consisted of compilations of articles from these.

"The Astrologer in the Nineteenth Century" was a collection of articles from "The Straggling Astrologer", published in 1825[i], and arranged according to topic. "The Familiar Astrologer" contained direct reproductions of various issues of magazines, and was collected from "Urania" and later magazines. It is cited by Godwin as "Composed in 1828, published in 1831"[ii]. Despite the prominence of astrology in their titles, these publications dealt with all aspects of occultism, and contain accounts of rituals, guides to divination, and articles on alchemy, among others. More of the articles are oriented towards popular folk magic and less toward high philosophy, although "high magic" is also represented . They also include more fiction and less instructions for stage magic than "The Conjuror's Magazine". "The Astrologer in the Nineteenth Century" features an account of a necromantic ritual that was published in Sibly's fourth part, reproduced here, along with the accompanying engraving of Edward Kelley and an associate raising a spirit. According to Davies[iii], in the early 19th century "The Astrologer in the Nineteenth Century" was the only affordable publication in Great Britain in print that resembled "The Magus".

Interestingly enough, it appears that Smith crossed paths with another group of occultists who were practicing in Great Britain at this time, who contributed material to his later publications. These went beyond what the manuscripts that Denley had access to contained, which Smith drew on heavily. Godwin recounts that in the eleventh issue of "The Straggling

---

i Godwin, 145
ii ibid., 147
iii Davies, "Grimoires", 137

Astrologer", in 1824, it's announced that a group called "The Mercurii" were now helping the editor out[i], and in the successor publication "Urania", the "The Mercurii" are listed as a collective contributor. Who these were is obscure, but Godwin provides evidence in the form of occult manuscripts published by a Smith that came from a known source other than Denley to suggest they really existed and were not wholly made up by Smith[ii].

"The Astrologer in the Nineteenth Century" had an interesting afterlife. The book was pirated by Laurens William de Laurence of Chicago in 1918 and retitled "The Old Book of Magic, a Precise History of its Procedure, Rites, and Mysteries", by "Raphael", and sold to through de Laurence's catalog. This catalog was unique in that it was aimed at the African American community, as well as the Carribean islands, with copies even making their way to Africa itself. However, it's not known how popular the book was or how many copies were sold. Unfortunately, even though both "The Astrologer in the Nineteenth Century" and "The Familiar Astrologer" were solid publications, and contained actual occult material, Smith later transitioned to the less seemly aspects of occult publishing. In this, he was indicative of the new trends in occult publishing that were emerging around his time.

After publishing his magazines and collections he followed up with "The Royal Book of Dreams" 1830[iii] and "The Lady-Witch of Raphael" 1831[iv]. Both of these presented material that had been gone over before in other manuals, and were packaged with either miraculous backstories to make them more appealing, or marketing that presented them as entertainment. The "Royal Book of Dreams" is mostly a manual for Geomancy, and only has one essay about dreams in the front. It was prefaced by a long tale relating how the manuscript was miraculously found by a construction worker in a pit after being buried for several centuries, and was bound in wood, a story that belongs more to the realm of supernatural fiction than fact. Considering that Smith's first book, "A Philosophical Merlin" was about Geomancy, that publication is a more likely precursor.

The second, "The Lady-Witch of Raphael", was "adapted to lay about in drawing-rooms, to be read in gardens and groves-to ornament the boudoir, for amusement in evening parties, as an innocent substitute

---

i Godwin, 144
ii ibid.,146
iii ibid.
iv ibid.

for cards". It contained supposedly factual, melodramatic, accounts of the supernatural both supposedly experienced by Raphael directly and by others, combined with poems, instructions on divination, and short, superficial, sections on other parts of popular occultism. The "Witch" aspect was intended as an evocative phrase, in a sense reminiscent of publications containing titles like "Teen Witch".

Hockley

Another of the people employed by Denley in the 1820s copying manuscripts was a very young Frederick Hockley[i]. Hockley would go on to be a primary source on magic for the more magically inclined members of the Societas Rosicruciae In Anglia, who would in turn be highly influential on, and indirectly responsible for founding, the Golden Dawn. Hockley was born in 1808, and may have started working at Denley's at the age of 18 in 1826, based on a statement in his presentation to the London Dialectical Society reproduced in Hamil's "The Rosicrucian Seer" that he began crystal gazing in 1826[ii]. Owen Davies in "Witchcraft, Magic, and Culture 1736-1951"[iii] quotes from a scrapbook by the astrologer E.Proctor that names Denley, Hockley, and Smith as members of "what amounted to a mutual aid society" of astrologers "between the years 1820 and 1850", with the date possibly being vague because of the difficulty of pinning down when the book was assembled. Several of the manuscripts known to have been copied by Hockley originated with Sibly, and the influence of Sibly's work, either directly or indirectly, and possibly that of the magical tradition that Sibly was a part of, is visible in Hockley's own writings. Material from one of Sibly's manuscripts was reproduced in Hockley's essay "Crystaliomancy, or the Art of Invoking Spirits by the Crystal", published in Hamil's "The Rosicrucian Seer"[iv] and more recently reprinted by Teitan Press.

Hockley's influence, the SRIA, and the Golden Dawn, and Sibly.

Before discussing Hockley and his successors, I should be clear that what I'm stating here is that Sibly and the circle around Denley in the 1820s influenced the worldview and understanding of magic that Hockley

---

i   Hamil, 11
ii ibid., 96
iii Davies, "Witchcraft, Magic, and Culture", 238
iv Hamil, 102

possessed, and that this worldview in turn was influential on some of the members of the SRIA who were interested in practical magic. However, while these members consulted Hockley and learned from him, their take on esotericism as a whole appears to have been much different from his, and reflected the times in which they lived in as opposed to those of Hockley's youth. Hockley had extensive contact with Francis Irwin and Kenneth R. Mackenzie, who are usually credited as being sources and influences, either directly or indirectly, of both the Golden Dawn and the cipher manuscript that served as its founding document, Westcott receiving the cipher manuscript from Mackenzie's widow.

The SRIA itself was not a magical organization but one devoted to research and discussion about all aspects of Rosicrucianism. Members would meet and present lectures, or papers, on different topics that they were looking into. It was a group whose members had a diverse range of interests both within "Rosicrucianism" and beyond it, the term being loosely defined. Irwin, Mackenzie, and a few others, had an interest in practical magic, yet they were in the minority. As Ellic Howe points out in his excellent "The Magicians of the Golden Dawn", a number of early SRIA members (including Irwin and Mackenzie)also had an interest in spiritualism, yet that didn't make the SRIA a spiritualist organization[i]. Beyond that, while Irwin stayed a member, Mackenzie left after having helped found it, being unsatisfied with it, rejoining much later in a non-official capacity. Despite this, Mackenzie remained a vital part of the occult world of Great Britain, and maintained friendships with many members of the SRIA. Mackenzie also fell out with Hockley[ii], although it's not clear why this was. Mackenzie's leaving points to another feature of the early SRIA: members joined who claimed to have had some sort of Rosicrucian initiation and then got into arguments with other members about who should have precedence in the organization, based on their supposed past affiliations. Yet, despite this early friction, the SRIA's role as a place of gathering for occultists to discuss issues they were all interested in provided the environment that lead to the Golden Dawn.

Hockley seems to have been seen by the more magically minded members of the SRIA as a kind of naïve rustic and who had links to the past. He was a real, live, magician, who had been employed by John Denley, and who was familiar with the old authors and works, and who even had pieces of gossip from back in the day. Despite this, casting Hockley as an

---

i Howe, 33
ii Hamil, 19

isolated, somewhat archaic, magician, is inaccurate. In point of fact his crystal scrying took place on the background of proto-spiritualism, and his interpretation of what he was doing was influenced at least in part by the thought of Emmanuel Swedenborg, an interest that was also broadly influential in the first half of the 19th century.

Hamill, in "The Rosicrucian Seer", reproduces an account of a speech given by Hockley at the meeting of the London Dialectical Society where Hockley outlines his experiences with spiritualism. He starts out by declaring that he's been a spiritualist for forty five years, and identifies his crystal scrying with the spiritualist movement proper.[i] In the question and answer session, Hockley cites William M. White's "Life of Swedenborg" as embodying what he believes to be the case on the issue of spirit doubles. Although at the same meeting, Hockley weighs in on another current occult interest by saying that he doesn't believe spiritualism has anything to with Mesmerism[ii], in many other documents reproduced by Hamil he approvingly cites the concept, as well as that of Somnabulism. "Somnabulism" was a mutation of Animal Magnetism into what's vulgarly called "Mesmerism", focussed on hypnotism, a development that was unique to Great Britain and whose origin is chronicled by Monod in "Solomon's Secret Arts"[iii]. In fact, Hockley minutely examines the relation of Swedenborg to Somnabulism, in the context of a review of a book on Animal Magnetism in the April 1850 edition of "The Zoist", reproduced in Hamil[iv]. I think it's safe to say that while Hockley was a believer in Animal Magnetism as well as Mesmerism, he was not an uncritical one[v]. In his contact with these belief systems, as well, Hockley was not out of touch with his times.

If this was the case in general, his actual method for crystal scrying was very much the opposite. Even though Hockley was not isolated from the mainstream of occultism of his time, what he did when he scryed with crystals, actually when his wife or partner scryed with crystals, was very much in line with ceremonial magic. The scrying took place after

---

i Hamil, 96
ii ibid. 97
iii Monod, 305
iv Hamil, 206

v The interaction between 19th and 18th century occultism in Hockley's thought is something that would profit from more analysis. Unfortunately, it is outside the scope of this book.

a highly ceremonial magical ritual[i], and Hockley's methods for doing this drew on sources that went far, far back in the tradition of British ceremonial magic.

As for the results of Hockley's crystal scrying, unfortunately, according to Hamil the whereabouts of many of the transcripts are unknown[ii], but a few extracts are preserved in the papers of Francis Irwin, who was loaned some of them by Hockley. The extracts include material that is quite similar to other spiritualist writings, both then and now, such as "Before the earth was made about 2,000 Angels were created, formed in the image of their maker, there was no distinction between them, they were angels of the highest order. When the Earth was made and the first man it was the intention of the Divine Master that the Angels have guardianship of those upon Earth and the whole generation of their offspring."[iii]

Hockley corresponded with Irwin extensively about spiritualist matters, and both Mackenzie and Irwin were believers, with Mackenzie reportedly stating after the demise of Eliphas Levi that he "would not be difficult to find" via a medium[iv]. Irwin's correspondence with Hockley shows Irwin to be both interested in the past and present of magic, in getting information on the more classical English writers on the occult while also exploring the more contemporaneous interests shared by himself and Hockley.

Hockley also considered himself a Rosicrucian[v], although precisely what he meant by this is unclear. Irwin thought enough of his Rosicrucianism induct him into the S.R.I.A., first waving the requirement that he attend a meeting to receive the grade of Zeleator, and then conferring on him the grade of Adeptus Exemptus,[vi] the highest possible for Irwin to grant. Although this was honorary, Hamil reports that Hockley did later join a regular S.R.I.A group, although he wasn't a regular attendee at its meetings[vii].

---

    i   Hamil, 105-106
    ii ibid., 109
    iii ibid., 119
    iv Godwin 219
    v   Hamil, 21-22
    vi Hamil, 18
    vii ibid., 19

Irwin was the originator of the "Fratres Lucis" or "Brotherhood of Light", a group founded on spiritualist communications[i], along with Mackenzie. Irwin claimed to be in spiritual contact with discarnate Rosicrucian masters, who gave the Fratres Lucis its doctrines[ii]. Hockley was a member as well[iii]. Irwin and Mackenzie were also members of the "Society of Eight", a group associated with alchemy and magical working that William Wynn Westcott, one of the founders of the Golden Dawn, would later join. Joscelyn Godwin points to both of these as being part of the "breeding ground" for the Golden Dawn[iv]. Hockley was also a member of the "Society of Eight", although his membership may have been more symbolic than actual[v].

Bringing things back around, Hockley's specific influence is hard to pick out in the works that became part of the Golden Dawn. One possible exception is a connection to the Cipher Manuscript itself through the geomantic figures in it, geomancy being a system of divination used both by Hockley and the circle around Denley. Hockley was a mentor to both Mackenzie and Irwin. Mackenzie was the source for the cipher manuscript, although his role in producing it is unclear. Both Irwin and Mackenzie knew Westcott through the SRIA and through the Society of Eight. Connecting this back with Sibly, we can say in turn that Hockley shared in Sibly's general worldview, although he modified it, and that there's a likelihood that some of the knowledge of magic that Hockley possessed either came from Sibly's manuscripts or was influenced by them, as well as by the general environment around Denley. Despite the indirect chain running from Sibly, through Denley, to Hockley, there are suggestions that certain occult beliefs Sibly subscribed to were ultimately passed onto the Golden Dawn, although it's impossible to know if they were simply 'in the air', or if there was a more concrete connection.

In the fourth part of "A New Illustrated Guide", there's a plate that contains four images illustrating the state of man before and after the fall. Sibly explains in the accompanying text that before the exile of man from the Garden of Eden, man was free from domination by elemental and planetary influences, but after the fall he was trapped by them. The illustrations draw on physiology and astrology to portray the state of man

---

i   Godwin, 219
ii ibid., 220
iii Hamil, 21
iv Godwin, 220
v   Hamil, 98

before and after the fall. The Golden Dawn's drawings portraying man before and after the fall parallel these, albeit transferring the idea from an astrological context into a Kabbalistic one, and situating man on the Tree of Life. This idea of the Fall involving the subjection of man to the elements may have been drawn by Sibly from the thought of Jacob Boehme, although the general idea can be found as far back as the Corpus Hermeticum.

Another point of similarity is the belief outlined by Sibly that Heaven and Hell aren't places that exist in physically different areas but are invisibly present at the same time on earth, all sharing the same space, along with the other spirit realms. In Sibly's presentation, these areas coexist but residents of the lower areas cannot perceive those of the higher areas. This belief can be traced in part to the doctrines of Swedenborg, who believed that many places, states and experiences in the afterlife were self-generated by beings rather than actual. However, interestingly enough, some of the material Sibly used to outline this belief comes from a source that predated Swedenborg by at least a hundred years. Taking that into account, it still parallels the Golden Dawn's idea that all of the spheres of the Tree of Life are simultaneously present here on earth.

Part II, The Work Itself

The current work is a compilation of four short pieces from the first part of Sibly's "A New and Complete Illustration of the Celestial Science of Astrology" plus the entire fourth part of the work entitled:

"Part the Fourth, Containing the Distinction between Astrology and the Wicked Practice of Exorcism. With a General Display of Witchcraft, Magic, and Divination, Founded Upon The Existence of Spirits Good and Bad, and their Affinity with the Affairs of this World."

"A New and Complete Illustration" is a very good presentation of astrology that draws from earlier sources and contains much information that could be applied to esoteric work. However, examining this material would take us very far afield. Instead, the selections presented here are those that deal more directly with Sibly's esoteric view of the universe and with magic. While the total number of pages in "A New and Complete Illustration" varied according to the edition, the one used here weighs in at 1127 pages split over two volumes.

The four short parts are William Lilly's letter "To a Young Student of Astrology", first published in "Christian Astrology"[i] and used without attribution, the poem "An Invocation of Urania" by Sibly, a selection from the introductory section of the first part, and the essay "A Summary View of the Works of Creation, in the Construction of Nature". All four shed light on Sibly's view of the world and round out some of the blanks in the material contained in the fourth part. Together, they make up about a quarter of the text of this volume.

The letter "To a Young Student of Astrology" deals with the spiritual and moral attitude an astrologer should have. It isn't exactly as printed in Christian Astrology. Sibly appears to have added a few sentences and deleted others, possibly in an attempt to make the style more contemporary. "An Invocation of Urania" is a poem about the muse of astrology. The selection from the beginning of part one illustrates Sibly's view of how astrology works in the context of the universe as a whole, drawing on both religious and naturalistic sources. It also outlines his concepts of "Time" and "Chance" and their relation to determinism in astrology. Because the aim here is not to present a justification of astrology as a whole, the rest of this essay, which goes into the subject in minute detail, has not been reproduced.

The fourth selection is a general survey of the physical and spiritual world that brings the focus away from astrology and towards the greater whole. It starts with an extended and detailed discussion of the elements, then touches on astrology before going into detail about how celestial influences are related to the heavenly realm, proofs of the existence of god, how the human body reflects the macrocosm, and the nature of angels. It ends with a brief presentation of the astrological world through the lens of the Kabbalah.

The fourth part of "A New Illustration", as opposed to the fourth selection from the first part, is divided into three sections. The first is devoted to an account of what happens after death, the spirit world, and specific information on the nature of Heaven and Hell, angels and demons. As Sibly states, this account is partially derived from Swedenborg, whom he quotes extensively, and also shows the influence of Jacob Boehme, especially in the section on the Fall of Man. There are also small biographies of John Dee, Edward Kelly, Apollonius of Tyana, Roger Bacon, and Paracelsus. This takes up about a third of the work.

---

i Lilly, xxxi

The second section is the synthesis of material from Reginald Scot's "The Discoverie of Witchcraft", Scot's essay "A Discourse on Divels and Spirits" that accompanied the original "Discoverie", material from an anonymous author added to the 1665 edition of the "Discoverie", and Sibly's own thought. This section deals with spirits, particular spirits, angels and demons, varieties of talismans and charms, magic, magical rituals, incense, as well as containing more information on the structure of the magical universe. It also includes a recipe by Sibly for alchemically extracting the spirit of plants and herbs.

The third and smallest part is a reproduction of a letter published by a paper in Sibly's home town of Bristol that recounts a cautionary tale of a man who experimented with magic and supposedly experienced terrible consequences.

"The Discoverie of Witchcraft"

The fourth part of Sibly's "A New Illustration" has been overlooked in part because of the claim that much of it is just plagiarized from Reginald Scot's "The Discoverie of Witchcraft". However, as we shall see, this is only partially true, and the story is more complicated than it might seem. In fact, far from being a disability, Sibly's use of the "Discoverie" is a key to one of the most interesting and valuable aspects of the work. To understand why this is, a few things need to be kept in mind.

First, the accusation of plagiarism of the "Discoverie" carries with it the implication that Sibly used material from a source that was hostile, or at least skeptical, to the practice of magic itself, and that because of this, it's not a reliable source. Despite exceptions like Agrippa's student Johann Weyer, most of the authors of books arguing for and against the idea of witchcraft were lawyers, priests, or scholars, who were not personally involved in magic. Scot himself was no magician and was skeptical both of the concept of magic and of much of the theology that allowed for its existence. However, a great deal of the material that Sibly quotes, that he plagiarizes outright, does not come from Scot himself but from an anonymous author who inserted two very large additions into the 1665 edition of the work. These additions are composed of a large essay on magic and nine chapters of practical instructions. Unlike Scot, the author of these anonymous sections did believe in magic, was a magician, and declared that he was inserting the material to correct some of the errors that Scot made in his presentation of the subject. Because this is the case,

Sibly is often not actually quoting a hostile or skeptical source but a practitioner of magic himself.

Second, as Owen Davies has shown[i], even though Scot's "Discoverie" was meant as a skeptical work to be used against self appointed 'witch finders', the original text contains so many documentary examples of charms, recipes, and magical workings that it was used by magical practitioners themselves. The "Discoverie" entered into the practical tradition of magic through this, and the additions to the 1665 edition were most likely made to help sell it to practitioners[ii].

Thirdly, the "Discoverie" as it's available in the United States is not the "Discoverie" that Sibly used. The version of the "Discoverie" in print in the U.S, issued by Dover Publications, is a reprint of the 1930 edition prepared by Montague Summers, who not only cut the anonymous additions but also deleted Scot's own essay "A Discourse on Divels and Spirits", which was contained in the original edition. The latter was most likely done because Summers disagreed with it's skeptical take on theology. In fact, the contents of the work as Sibly saw it are only fully contained in the 1665 edition, a critical edition based on it that was produced by Brinsley Nicholson in 1886, a rare reprint of the Nicholson version from 1976, and a recent hand bound reprint of the same that's even rarer. Joseph Peterson's otherwise excellent website, "The Esoteric Archives", only reproduces the parts of the extra material that contain ritual elements, and skips over the more philosophical parts entirely, also skipping all of Scot's original "Discourse on Divels and Spirits". Besides out of print hardcopies, the only other readily available sources for versions that have all the material Sibly had access to are an online copy of Nicholson hosted by archive.org and a pay per download pdf copy of the 1665 edition hosted by the "Conjuring Arts Research Center" at "http://www.conjuringarts.org/", a resource for stage magicians. This has no doubt made it more difficult to check Sibly's work against the original to see what is and is not actually there.

On the issue of Sibly's plagiarism, it's important to remember that not only was he a practicing magician himself, but he came to magic from a popular background, not an elite one, although he would later professionalize himself. The services he offered, such as astrological readings, and medicine making use of both of herbalism and astrology, overlapped with the same types of services cunning people supplied.

---

   i   Davies, "Cunning Folk", 124-125, 134
   ii   ibid., 127

These, in turn, were a large portion of the practitioners who made use of the "Discoverie" for magical purposes. Interestingly enough, Davies records[i] that a copy of Sibly's "A New Illustration" was found in the library of a family of Welsh cunning folk in the 19th century. It's possible, and I think very likely, that Sibly was citing this information not simply out of convenience or plagiarism but because he at some point had contact with the mostly Christian cunning craft tradition that made use of the "Discoverie" as a source text. Because of this, it may have also reflected his own worldview as a magical practitioner. Additionally, Sibly, at some point in his life, actually owned at least one manuscript from a tradition of grimoires that Scot himself used to compile his "Discoverie", which lies outside of the familiar grimoire series like the "Lemegeton", the "Key of Solomon", and the "Grimoirum Verum" families, and was unpublished until a few years ago[ii].

It's also worth noting that Sibly did not simply take the whole text from the 1665 edition and market it as his own. Instead, he took paragraphs and pages from different sections of the work, from those authored both by Scot as well as by the anonymous contributor, reworked them in some cases, and often put them together in new sequences. These edits appear to have been made to try to concentrate disparate material from all the different sections according to subject matter. Though most of Sibly's quotations come from the anonymous additions and from Scot's "Discourse", he also quotes extensively from the original edition's fifteenth book, and there are bits and pieces from other places in the original "Discoverie" that make their way in, such as a paragraph from book nine about Solomon and prophecy.

Though Sibly marketed the work as completely his own, there is also an extensive tradition in occultism of taking previous works, editing and compiling them for one's own use, and putting them under one's own name. Not only that, but scholarship in up until the end of the Renaissance in general was fuzzy on the difference between compilation and original authorship, at least when it was supposed to be for a reference work, as opposed to a treatise. I believe that much, but certainly not all, of what Sibly did falls into these categories.

---

i   Davies, "Cunning Folk", 135
ii In "The Book of Treasure Spirits", Rankine ed.

Before dealing with the issue of Sibly's own presentation of the material in the fourth part, and what his own stance on it might have been, it's useful to review in more detail just what unfamiliar material the 1665 edition contained.

The Discoverie's Contents

First, there's Scot's original essay "A Discourse on Divels and Spirits", from 1584. Scot's "Discourse" serves as a conclusion to the "Discoverie" and is remarkably enlightened for its time. It doesn't examine popular material, but takes on the theology and philosophy of the witch finders and anti-magic theologians, ridiculing them and picking apart their arguments. Scot wearily recounts all of the different opinions they have about things like the Fall of Satan and the nature of Devils, then condemns all of it for its incoherence and implausibility. Strikingly, the information Sibly uses from Scot's "Discourse" are opinions that Scot recounts in detail as being false. Overall, Scot's essay is smart, entertaining, and humorous, and well aware of the follies of his subject.

The anonymous additions are divided into a philosophical portion and a practical one. The first was included as a second book of "A Discourse", while the practical part is composed of nine extra chapters added to the beginning of book fifteen. Scot's original text of book fifteen starts after it at chapter ten. The two new pieces are linked, the theoretical part referring the reader to the practical chapters for more detail about what's being described. The second book of "A Discourse" is a self contained essay on the nature of magic and of the spirit world, and as a piece of literature it's a serious presentation of the author's worldview. The authors declare that they want to set the record straight on what Scot got wrong about the magical world and proceed to outline just what they think is the truth of the matter. The anonymous author states at the beginning:

"Because the Author in his foregoing Treatise, upon the Nature of Spirits and Devils, hath only touched the subject thereof superficially, omitting the more material part; and with a brief and cursory Tractat, hath concluded to speak the least of this subject which indeed requires most amply to be illustrated ; therefore I thought fit to adjoyn this subsequent discourse; as succedaneous to the fore-going, and conducing to the compleating of the whole work."[i]

---

i Nicholson, 492

It should be noted that although the anonymous author mentions witches in passing, he or she does not refer to himself as such, but simply implies that he's either a magician who performs evocations, or is acting on behalf of a group of them.

The other addition, the nine chapters added to book fifteen, resemble a grimoire, and give information such as how to consecrate implements, how to evoke spirits, as well as accounts of evocations. The rituals they provide are much more fully detailed than those reproduced in the original "Discoverie". Book fifteen in the original "Discoverie" was the section that included most of the accounts of what could be called high magic, and the new material fits in with the old, albeit possessing a non-skeptical viewpoint. The contents of the added chapters to book fifteen of the "Discoverie", as well as that of the second book of the "Discourse", can perhaps be best gleaned by looking at their chapter titles.

Those of the second book of the "Discourse" are as follows:

Chapter I: "Of Spirits in General; What they are and how to be considered: Also how farr the power of Magitians and Witches is able to operate in Diabolical Magick".

Chap. II "Of the Good and Evil Daemons or Genii: Whether they are; what they are, and how they are manifested; also of their names, power, faculties, offices; how they are to be considered".

Chap III. "Of the Astral Spirits of men departed: What they are: And why they appear again: and what Witchcraft may be wrought by them."

Chap IV. "Of Astral Spirits or separate Daemons in all their distinctions, names, and natures, and places of Habitation, and what may be wrought by their Assistance. "

Chap V. "Of the Infernal Spirits, or Devils and damned Souls treating, what their Natures, Names, and Powers are, &c."

Chap. VI "Treating of the Nature, Force and Forms of Charms, Periapts, Amulets, Pentacles, Conjurations, Ceremonies, &c.",

Chap VII "Being the Conclusion of the Whole; wherein divers antient Spells, Charms, Incantations and Exorcisms are briefly spoken of."

The titles of the nine chapters added to Book Fifteen of the "Discoverie" are:

Chap I. "Of Magical Circles, and the reason of their Institution",

Chap II. "How to raise up the Ghost of one that hath hanged himself",

Chap III "How to raise up the three spirits, Paymon, Bathin, and Barma: And what wonderful things may be effected through their assistance."

Chap IV. "How to Consecrate all manner of Circles, Fumigations, Fire, Magical Garments, and Utensils."

Chap. V. "Treating more practically of the Consecrations of Circles, Fires, Garments, and Fumigations."

Chap VI. "How to raise and exorcise all sorts of Spirits belonging to the Airy Region."

Chap VII. "How to obtain the familiarity of the Genius or Good Angel, and cause him to appear".

Chap VIII. "A form of Conjuring Luridan, the Familiar, otherwise called Belelah."

Chap. IX. "How to Conjure the Spirit Balkin the Master of Luridan".

Sibly's own view in the Fourth Part.

The plagiarism of Scot's work as well as that of the anonymous author prompts the question of what exactly was Sibly's own attitude towards the material contained in the fourth part? Did he really believe in it, and if he believed in it, did he agree with its many condemnations of magic?

The first question can be partially answered by looking at the material from the beginning of "A New Illustration" included in this book, particularly the fourth short selection from the first part. While not identical to the perspective contained in the fourth part, it's certainly compatible with it, to the point where Godwin believed that the fourth part was authored by Sibly, though he comments that Sibly's perspective was "anything but emancipated"[i]. The second question can be answered as follows.

The subtitle of the fourth part states that its purpose is to show how astrology is not like these other types of occultism. However, Sibly doesn't actually address the question at all. Indeed, there's really no argument made, just a catalog of occult information. Though much of the magical material is framed by warnings telling the reader not to do it, Sibly gives information on how to conjure spirits and what incense to use. As more than one commentator has noted, his protestations about the wickedness of the material wears thin, considering that he includes so much of it. However, I don't believe Sibly was wholly hypocritical in his cautions to the reader.

The majority of magical practices he condemns, either through quotes from the "Discoverie", the "Discourse", or his own words, have to do with calling up evil spirits. As for good spirits, he not only reproduces a list of seven of the chief ones (along with the corresponding infernal ones), such as Nalgah, taken from the second book of the "Discourse", but he reproduces the sigils of three of them, and lists the things they can help a person with. Natural magic, under which astrology falls, is defended in full. For this Sibly simply reproduces the section from the anonymous author of the second book of the "Discourse" defending making talismans and amulets using natural magic, with few alterations. Sibly also quotes approvingly the anonymous sections from the "Discoverie" and the "Discourse" that deal with elemental spirits, listing them as neither good nor bad, just not immortal.

Sibly also makes quite a lot of positive remarks about the "Good Genius" in the part of the text that contains most of his original writing, going so far as to quote a section from book nine of Scot's "Discoverie" that suggests that Solomon himself got his wisdom from a spirit. He also suggests that the pagan gods of old who communicated to people via oracles were really formerly human spirits. Not only that, but he clarifies himself by saying that Plato and others believed that the spirits of good men appeared to other good men in order to advise them, and goes even farther by saying that their theurgic rituals were intended to attract these spirits in order to talk to them.

Indeed, one full page of the illustrations of the fourth part is devoted to portraits of people who he identifies as having received inspiration from spirits, genius', or angels. He calls these the "Order of Inspirati".

---

i   Godwin 109

The portraits that appear are those of Apollonius of Tyana, Roger Bacon, John Dee, the prophet Mohammad, Edward Kelly, and Paracelsus. The arrangement appears to be divided into an approved group and a less accepted one, with the more accepted Apollonius of Tyana, Roger Bacon, and John Dee appearing on the left and Mohammad, Edward Kelly, and the rascally Paracelsus appearing on the right. John Dee, in the short biography, is lauded as being a very good individual and a great scholar, despite his questionable angelic communications. Sibly states that the forces that presented themselves to Dee and Kelley lied about being angels, but attributes the confusion to Edward Kelly, who is presented as a person who lead the good doctor astray. Sibly then goes on to cast Kelley as being increasingly corrupt in his magical practices after Dee kicked him out, making Kelley's life into a cautionary tale.

I believe Sibly was doing two things in presenting the fourth part of "A New Illustration" in the manner he did. On the one hand, it's my opinion that he honestly did believe that certain practices were dangerous for the public to toy with, and were best left alone. On the other, I believe he acted out of a desire to present occult material to the public while preserving his own image as a respectable figure. Even though the Enlightenment had opened up room for discussion on topics that would otherwise have been taboo, there were still limits. In his life after "A New Illustration", Sibly professionalized himself by obtaining an MD, and attempted to justify his occult medical beliefs to the mainstream of medical practice. Having a stain on his reputation such as openly endorsing occult practices would have been an inconvenient obstacle to accomplishing that goal.

Still, despite all this, it's impossible to know just by looking at the material contained in the fourth part how Sibly viewed it, beyond the indications just cited, and that he was prepared to claim it as his own. Fortunately, there's a recently published source that can shed some light on the question. Joseph Peterson and Ibis Press have published a facsimile and transcribed edition[i] of a set of manuscripts made by Frederick Hockley that in turn contain several manuscripts, one large and one small, that originate with Sibly. In particular, the larger manuscript, a version of the Greater Key of Solomon, contains a preface by Sibly about the nature of magic itself. These manuscripts weren't intended for the public eye, and while Sibly might have been sensitive to the beliefs and preferences of grimoire buyers, he would have had much less reason to mince words

---

i   As "The Clavis or Key to the Magic of Solomon"

about magic in order to preserve his reputation. The manuscripts open up a world that, in the words of Lewis Carroll, gets "Curiouser and Curiouser".

The Clavis

The "Clavis or Key to the Magic of Solomon" reproduced by Peterson contains three manuscripts. The first is a translation of a French version of the Key of Solomon in the same 'family' as the main one translated by Skinner & Rankine in "The Veritable Key of Solomon". This contains the preface on spirituality and magic by Sibly. The second is a combination of an account of four experiments evoking spirits, which will be addressed in the next section, and a presentation of Sibly's "Rotalo" or "Wheel of Wisdom", which is a wheel dealing with astrological correspondences. The third manuscript is a text by Hockley entitled "The Complete Book of Magical Science".

Even though Peterson doubts that Sibly wrote the Preface, or was involved with any other part of the manuscript[i], there's little reason to think this is the case. That the preface cites Jacob Boehme is not a disability but a sign that it really is by him. Sibly's work was influenced by Boehme, as Monod writes[ii], and if use of the concept of "Anima Mundi" is any indication, Boehminist thought also permeated Sibly's later medical works, as shown by Debus[iii]. That there was interest in Boehme's philosophy in England at the time of Sibly is amply documented in chapter seven of Monod's "Solomon's Secret Arts"[iv]. Also, the style, tone, and content match the first section of the fourth part, which Sibly had a greater hand in composing. It's viewpoint also broadly conforms with the material included from the "Discoverie" and the "Discourse", although the moralistic tone is mostly missing. There is some evidence of commercial exploitation by the copiers of the manuscript in that a partial copy of the drawings of the magical instruments from the fourth part is inserted even though they're not actually used. The magic circle reproduced at the end of the manuscript that deals with constructing magic rings is significantly different from that reproduced in the other drawings.

---

    i   Peterson, xii
    ii   Monod, 275-276
    iii Debus, 263
    iv Especially pages 247-254

Overall, though, there are more similarities between the preface and other works by Sibly than differences. His overall approach is unique and different from that of the fourth part in that he explicitly quotes and uses Jacob Boehme's writings as a guide to magical operations. Strangely enough, this is not out of character for Boehme. While it may not be widely known, magic appears to be repeatedly cited with approval by Boehme in his writings. Examples of this include "The Signature of All Things" and "The Clavis", the latter of which Sibly quotes[i]. The other works of Boehme that Sibly cites in his preface are "Forty Questions on the Soul" and "The Threefold Life of Man".

Sibly preserves some of the distinctions outlined in the fourth part, approving of natural magic and working with benevolent and good spirits, but he modifies the definition of what counts as illicit dealing with evil spirits quite a bit. After outlining Boehme's philosophy, and suggesting a course of self preparation a magician should undergo before working, Sibly presents six different methods of magic, three general subdivisions these fall into, then some tips aimed specifically at magicians who are Christian, which is somewhat misleading. Let's start by looking at the second method of magic, which is worth quoting in full:

"Secondly. Magical purposes are brought about by invocation to God alone, this is partly Prophetical, and Philosophical, and partly as it were Theophrastical, other things there are, which by reason of the True God, are done with the Princes of Spirits, that his desires may be fulfilled, such is the work of the Mercurialist"[ii]

In listing "Prophetical, Philosophical" and "Theophrastical", purposes, Sibly is likely talking about theurgy and other purely devotional practices. "Theophrastical" literally means "Divine Expression", in the sense of speech (as well as being Paracelsus' self given title). "Mercurialist" is taken from alchemy, and likely refers in a metaphorical way to wielding the power of the Philosophical Mercury to command spirits. The key phrase in the definition, though, is "with the Princes of Spirits".

"The Princes of Spirits" does not refer to angels, who would be listed as such and not commanded, and it doesn't refer to elemental spirits, because Sibly lists working with them as another type of magic. Instead, it refers to the Princes of the four directions, which most grimoires and works such as Agrippa's "Three Books of Occult Philosophy", refer to as the Demon Kings of the four directions. This is very important in that

---

i Peterson, 5-6
ii Peterson, 10-11

beyond Sibly stating that it's okay to work with demons themselves, many grimoires place the spirits the magician can evoke under one of the four Kings or Princes, meaning that theoretically it's permissible to work with these subordinate demons as well. This would jibe with Sibly's ownership of the Lemegeton, a copy of the demonic sigils of which Skinner and Rankine reproduce in "The Goetia of Dr. Rudd" as an appendix[i]

In the context of his discussion on Boehme, and his later advice to magicians, Sibly appears to have believed that if a magician is pious, meditates on God in an esoteric way, and then calls on the spirits for a use he feels is necessary, the operation could be seen as an extension and realization of God's will in the world, and its success a victory of good against evil. Surely, a pure desire would further that. Although it is somewhat speculative, Sibly may also have thought that by commanding evil spirits for good purposes you could help them. In the Swedenborgian doctrine, demons and angels can change, and, theoretically, a demon could repent. That the power to command them is listed in the same category as, though not identical to, appeal to "God alone" is important in the context of the later statements about the power of Christ in magic.

After outlining the six kinds of magic, Sibly lists three categories of operations that these can fall into, which are also very revealing. These are appealing to "God alone" for magic, using spirits that voluntarily come to you, and then using magic that is vaguely listed as being particularly Christian. From the context, it's clear that what this refers to is using the power of Christ to compel spirits to work with you involuntarily. The spirits that you would have to do this to would be evil spirits, or demons, that the magician was compelling to obey his commands. This is proved because after introducing the subject, he goes on to devote two whole manuscript pages to special preparations necessary for those who want to engage in these practices. In these, he stresses self purification, and again the importance of a good will, stating that if you use this power for bad purposes you will bring ruin on yourself. These preparations are done to make it easier for the magician to wield the power of Christ. After the warnings, he concludes by saying:

"But if, on the Contrary he is willing to do Justice, loves Mercy, and walks humbly with his God, he shall be Divinely Defended from all evil, and by joining his understanding to any Good Spirit, may produce what he will for all things are possible to them that Believe."[ii]

---

i   Skinner & Rankine, "The Goetia of Dr. Rudd", 402-403
ii Peterson, 14-15

There would be no reason to engage in all of this purificatory work or take these precautions if the magician was simply going to work with good or neutral spirits. Neither would he or she have to compel them by the power of Christ.

Interestingly enough, one of the types of magic that he outright disapproves of involves working with evil spirits without the power of Christ:

"But some make use of an opposite Magic, by which actions are produced by the Chief of the Evil Spirits, such were they who wrought by the Minor Gods of the Heathen"[i].

This should be taken in the context of what was just stated. This criteria does rule out some types of grimoire work, though. For instance, all work with the the Verum family would be forbidden.

Other than that, his definition of what's permissible is fairly open, provided that the magician is pious and using magic for a good purpose. That many of the talismans in the Key that follows the preface are for purposes that are less than disinterested perhaps points to the flexibility of the notion of a "good purpose". Notably, there's no mention of implicit pacts in working with spirits, a concept very beloved by the witch finders, and also something that gets a very heavy treatment in the fourth part. The grimoire itself, after Sibly's preface, also dismisses the idea of pacts[ii], and Sibly does nothing to challenge this.

I don't think that there is really any basic incompatibility between the position outlined by Sibly in the fourth part of "A New Illustration" and that outlined in his preface to the "Clavis". The point of view of in the latter is that magic dealing with evil spirits is very dangerous to engage in, needs special preparations, and requires the magician to be religiously devout. It also requires the magician to use it for a "good purpose". Taking this as indicative of Sibly's beliefs on the subject, the condemnation of working with evil spirits in the fourth part can be seen as a precaution against people who, in Sibly's view, were not sufficiently prepared to do so. Yet, even if that is the case, it remains a mystery why Sibly included much material that could be used just for that. There are other mysteries in the text of the preface as well.

A very strange coincidence happens on the second page. On it, there's a description of what happens to people after they pass on, declaring that spirits have a decreasing amount of energy that they draw on, and disappear

---

i   ibid., 11
ii Peterson, 18

when it is exhausted. The passage is listed in the preface as coming from Jacob Boehme's "Forty Questions on the Soul"[i], but the same idea also occurs in the anonymous second book of the "Discourse", added in 1665, where it's attributed to Paracelsus[ii].

The second set of manuscripts in Peterson's "Clavis" suggests that Sibly's relationship to the material in the "Discoverie" may have been much more intimate.

The Four Experiments Manuscript.

The "Four Experiments" manuscript reproduced in Peterson's "Clavis" provides evidence that Sibly had access to grimoire material from the same family that Scot used in compiling the original "Discoverie" in 1584. Circumstances around the manuscript suggest that practices related to it, and through it to the source used in the "Discoverie", were engaged in by those in Sibly's immediate circle, as well as those in his more distant circle.

The "Four Experiments" manuscript was bound up with a smaller one, the "Wheel of Wisdom", and both are reproduced in Peterson's "Clavis". The "Four Experiments" consist of accounts of evoking the spirits Birto, Vassago, Agares, and Bealpharos, as well as instructions for doing the same. The smaller manuscript is a copy of Sibly's "Rotalo" or "Wheel of Wisdom", a wheel of astrological correspondences, with a text by Sibly that explains how to use the wheel to make magical powders. It's likely that John Denley put the two texts together, with Hockley acting as the copyist. That the "Four Experiments" manuscript reproduced in the "Clavis" was owned by Sibly is suggested not just by the inclusion of the "Wheel of Wisdom" but also by the existence of a duplicate copy labeled as "Transcribed from the Autograph of Dr. Sibly". R.A. Gilbert lists this in his contribution to "The Rosicrucian Seer"[iii], without naming its owner, providing more information about the copy, such as that the "Four Experiments" are listed as being by "T.W.", and that the manuscript also contained a "Fragment of a translation of a very rare German MS Concerning Divine Magic. [and] Dr. Pistor, Introduction to the Theory of Cabala." in addition to the other texts.

---

  i ibid., 3
  ii Nicholson, 501
  iii Hamil, 31

"The Experiment of Bealpharos" was used by Scot to produce "An Experiment of Bealphares", contained in chapter 13 and 14 of book fifteen of "The Discoverie of Witchcraft"[i]. This was transcribed from an unknown copy of a manuscript in the same family as that of Sibly's "Four Experiments". While the same material showing up in the "Discoverie" and Sibly's copy could be dismissed as a fluke, or as Sibly plagiarizing the "Discoverie", and not really indicating continuity, the same material shows up in another copy of the "Experiments", contained in Sloane Manuscript 3824 and recently published by David Rankine as "The Book of Treasure Spirits", where it's published as "A Conjuration of Bealpharos". Both Sibly's "Four Experiments" and that in the "Book of Treasure Spirits" are much more extensive than the text contained in the "Discoverie", and that in "The Book of Treasure Spirits" dates from the 17th century, over a hundred years before the "Clavis" manuscript was made. Both texts line up with each other and with that reproduced in the "Discoverie", although the manuscript in "The Book of Treasure Spirits" is the most complete of them. That copy also proves that Scot got his information from the manuscripts, not the manuscripts from Scot.

The evidence that Scot transcribed "An Experiment of Bealphares" from a manuscript, and not the other way around, has to do with the clarity of the text.

The text of one of the invocations in "The Conjuration of Bealpharos" is reproduced with spelling errors in the "Discoverie"'s copy. This is important because the clean invocation from Rankine's text contains names that can be recognized as those that appear in other magical material, while many of those in the "Discoverie" are somewhat confused. It's unlikely that someone could have read Scot's copy and turned his names into the more familiar ones, and more likely that Scot, either intentionally or through carelessness, reproduced the names in a flawed way from a common manuscript ancestor.

Here are the differences: In the "Discoverie" the text is "Helie, helyon, esseire, Deus aeturnus, eloy, clemens, heloye, Deus sanctus, sabaoth, Deus exercituum, adonay, Deus mirabillis, iao, verax, anepheneton, deus ineffabilis, soldoy, dominatur dominus, on fortissimus, deus, qui, "[ii]

---

i Summers, 240-244
ii Summers, 242

The "Book of Treasure Spirits" conjuration reads: "Elie, Elion, Escherie, Deus, Eternus, Eloy, Elemens, Deus sanctus, Sabaoth, Deus Exercituum, Adonay, Deus mirabillis, Iao, Verax, Anepheketon, Deus Ineffabillis, Saday, Dominatur Dominus, On fortissimus, Agla, On, Tetragrammaton, Alpha & Omega"[i]

The significant differences are as follows, the "Discoverie" version first and the "Book of Treasure Spirits" second: 'Helie, Elie;' 'Helyon, elyon;' ' esserie, Escherie;' 'clemens, Elemens;' 'solday, Saday;'

Combined with Sibly's extensive citations of the "Discoverie" in the fourth part, this gives one pause.

While Peterson comments in his introduction to the "Clavis" that Scot's text of the "Experiment of Bealpharos" is considerably different than that reproduced in his text, this is only partially true[ii]. In point of fact the beginning of the "Clavis" manuscript is identical to that contained in the "Discoverie", and the beginning of the "The Book of Treasure Spirits" is the same as well. The section includes the drawings of the knife and its characters reproduced both in the "Discoverie" and Sibly's fourth part, and the instructions on how to use them. The unique magical circle that appears in the "Discoverie", which is a square with a circle inside of it, and another square inside of that, also appears in both the "Clavis" and Rankine's manuscript, although if they derived it from Scot or Scot derived it from a common ancestor manuscript is an open question.

What Scot does not include from the manuscript are the specific instructions for the magical work that goes beyond the common beginning section that is present in all three copies. After that section, he includes a text from a completely different source, and in place of the very extensive and particular instructions for evocations he places ones that are very generic, and don't include any holy names. The invocation from the "Book of Treasure Spirits" is inserted by Scot into the unrelated text, which has nothing to do with its original purpose[iii]. In the Sloane manuscript that invocation is part of a consecration ritual for a magical girdle to be used in calling up the spirit[iv]. This invocation does not appear in the "Clavis" manuscript.

---

    i   Rankine, "The Book of Treasure Spirits", 136-137
    ii   Peterson, x-xi
    iii Summers, 242
    iv Rankine, 136-137

The area that links the "Four Experiments" manuscript to practice deals with calling spirits into crystals. All the "Experiments" manuscripts contain references to drawing spirits into crystals, and Scot also deals with the subject in the chapter of the "Discoverie" titled "How to enclose a spirit in a christall stone"[i], which is directly before "An Experiment of Bealphares". Although the text is different from the "Experiments", it's here that the famous circle from the "Discoverie" makes its first appearance, albeit with additions for that particular ritual. Hockley, in his text "Crystaliomancy, or the Art of Invoking Spirits by the Crystal"[ii] also includes the "Discoverie" circle, though again it's impossible to tell what source he got the circle from, as well as long direct quotations from the "Four Experiments" manuscript, specifically from "The Experiment of Vassago"[iii] [iv]. Hockley's text, in effect, puts the two parts back together. This suggests that the material from the manuscript was not only copied but used as well. Crystal scrying was a common theme in the occult world around Sibly and Denley, with both Barrett and Parkins participating in it as well. Hockley's text on "Crystaliomancy" is reproduced in Hamil's "The Rosicrucian Seer" and has recently been published by The Teitan Press.

So what does this mean? While it's impossible to say just when Sibly acquired this manuscript, or if he had it before he wrote the fourth part of "A New Illustration", it suggests that a tradition that used it existed two hundred years after Scot's original publication of the "Discoverie", and Sibly had access to it. That the texts were still being used is pointed to by Hockley's use of the same manuscripts for his core work of crystal scrying. Sibly had the unique perspective of both publishing material from the "Discoverie" and owning texts descended from those that the "Discoverie" was compiled from. It also points to at least some texts in the "Discoverie" being more or less accurate references to magical practices that were current at Scot's time and that continued for quite a while. Rankine, in his introduction to the Sloane manuscript in "The Book of Treasure Spirits" links these practices to those of the aristocratic angel magic of the 17th century through the provenance of the manuscript.

The provenance of Sloane Manuscript 3824 takes things to another level. Rankine traces it from Hans Sloane, who donated his collection of manuscripts to the British Museum, to Joseph Jekyll, to John Somers. As

---

i   Summers, 238
ii Hamil, 103
iii Peterson, 196
iv Hamil, 106

Rankine says, Somers was the Lord Chancellor of England[i]. He served as this under William the III after the Glorious Revolution of 1688 which overthrew James II, which he also participated in the planning and execution of. It seems that a hundred years after the publication of Scot's "Discoverie" one of the most important men in England had a manuscript of the same material that Scot made use of. Remarkably, this was the same material that would make it's way to the humble Hockley, who incorporated some of it into his instructions for consecrating crystals used in scrying. It's a good argument against seeing Hockley as a rustic magician with no forebears. It also points to the interchange between traditions of 'high magic' and 'low magic' in England, from the 16th century to the early 19th, a phenomenon also mentioned by Davies[ii]. Finally, it points to the participation by Sibly, at some point in his life, in circles that may have been connected to those that produced the Sloane Manuscript, and that may themselves have been descended from the same circles that produced the manuscript Scot drew on in compiling "The Discoverie of Witchcraft".

Conclusion

Sibly's work provides a unique window into the world of a ceremonial magician in the late 18th century, before the Golden Dawn and the Theosophical Society came into existence. Sibly is an overlooked figure who drew on the thought of the 17th century, as well as the scientific thought of his day. He used both in a quixotic quest to prove to the world that the occult worldview of the 17th century was still relevant, and that it could still be used to explain contemporary scientific discoveries. His work was a blend of high magic from the aristocratic tradition, occult philosophy, and low magic from the popular tradition. The new esoteric thought of his day, such as that of Swedenborg and Mesmer, also played a role. His writing presents a way into the world of the occult that existed before the break between science and magic became permanent, before things bifurcated into the supernatural world, on the one hand, and the normal, sober, world of science on the other. The categories of "normal" and "paranormal" are not present in Sibly's work. Instead, everything can be explained by a common mechanism behind both that explains it all. For people looking for insight into the grimoire tradition, they could do worse.

---

i Rankine, 20
ii Davies, "Cunning Folk",72-73

For those interested in occultism during Sibly's time the best sources are "The Theosophical Enlightenment" by Joscelyn Goodwin and "Solomon's Secret Arts", a recent publication by Paul Monod. Owen Davies book "Cunning Folk" contains important information about the world of occult publishing in the late 18th century, as does his work "Grimoires", which also covers the later developments of popular occult publishing.

Works Cited:

Davies, Owen. Cunning Folk, Popular Magic in English History. London: Hambledon and London, 2003.

Davies, Owen. Grimoires, A History of Magical Books. New York:Oxford University Press, 2009.

Davies, Owen. Witchcraft, Magic and Culture, 1736-1951. New York: Manchester University Press, 1999.

Debus, Allen "Scientific Truth and Occult Tradition: The Medical World of Ebenezer Sibly (1751-1799)", Medical History vol. 26, 1982, 259-278. Electronic copy.

Godwin, Joscelyn. The Theosophical Enlightenment. Albany NY USA.:State University of New York Press, 1992.

Hamil, John. The Rosicrucian Seer, Magical Writings of Frederick Hockley,Great Britain: The Aquarian Press, 1986.

Howe, Ellic. The Magicians of the Golden Dawn, Ann Arbor MI USA: Samuel Weiser Inc., 1984.

King, Francis X. The Flying Sorcerer. United Kingdom:Mandrake, 1992.

Lilly, William. Christian Astrology, An Introduction to Astrology. The Resolution of all manner of Questions and Demands, Books 1 & 2. United States:Astrology Classics, 2004.

Monod, Paul Kléber. Solomon's Secret Arts, The Occult in the Age of Enlightenment. New Haven CT USA:Yale University Press, 2013.

Nicholson, Brinsely, ed., Reginald Scot. The Discoverie of Witchcraft by Reginald Scot. United Kingdom: Eliot Stock, 1886.

Peterson, Joseph. The Clavis or Key to the Magic of Solomon. Lakeland FL USA: Ibis Press, 2009.

Rankine, David. The Book of Treasure Spirits. United Kingdom: Avalonia, 2009.

Rankine, David, and Stephen Skinner. The Goetia of Dr. Rudd. Singapore: Golden Hoard Press, 2007.

Rankine, David, and Stephen Skinner. The Veritable Key of Solomon. Singapore: Llewellyn Publications, 2008.

Schuchard, Marsha Keith. "Rediscovering William "Hurricane" Gilbert: A Lost Voice of Revolution and Madness in the Worlds of Blake and the Romantics", BARS Conference:"Romantic Revelations," University of Keele, July 1999, Internet, http://www.williamgilbert.com/GILBERT_Schuchard.htm, accessed June 2014.

Summers, Montague, ed., Reginald Scot. The Discoverie of Witchcraft by Reginald Scot: with an introduction by the Rev. Montague Summers. USA: Dover Publications Inc., 1972.

TO THE
YOUNG STUDENT in ASTROLOGY.

My Friend,

WHOEVER thou art, that shalt with so much ease receive the benefit of my laborious studies, and dost intend to proceed in acquiring this heavenly knowledge of the Stars, wherein the great and admirable works of the invisible and all-glorious God are so manifestly apparent, in the first place consider and adore thy omnipotent CREATOR, and be thankful unto him for thy existence. Be humble, and let no natural knowledge, how profound and transcendent soever it be, elate thy mind, or withdraw thee from thy duty to that divine Providence, by whose all-seeing order and appointment, all things heavenly and earthly have their constant and never-ceasing motion; but the more thy knowledge is enlarged by this comprehensive science, the more do thou magnify the power and wisdom of the Almighty God, and drive to preserve thyself in his favour; having in constant remembrance, that the more holy thou art, and the nearer thou approached to God in thy religious duties, the purer judgment shalt thou always give. Beware of pride and self-conceit, yet never forget thy dignity. Reflect often on the primeval date of thy creation, that thou wast formed in the perfect image of God, and that no irrational creature durst offend Man, the *Microcosm,* but did faithfully serve and obey him, so long as he was master of his reason and passions, or until he suffered his own Free-Will to be governed by the unreasonable part. But alas! when the first father of us all gave up the reins to his disobedient affections, and deserted his reason and his God, then every creature and beast of the field became rebellious and disobedient to his command. Stand fast then, O Man ! to thy integrity, and thy religion ! consider thy own nobleness, and that all created things, both present and to come, were for thy sake created; nay, for thy sake, even God became man! Thou art that creature, who, being conversant with Christ, lived and conversest above the heavens. How many privileges and advantages hath God bestowed on thee ! thou ranged above the heavens by contemplation, and conceivest the motion and magnitude of the Stars; thou talked: with angels; yea, with God himself: thou hast all creatures within thy dominion, and keepest the Devils in subjection. Thy capacity for acquiring knowledge is unlimited by thy Maker; and the blessedness of an enlightened mind will bring thee the consolations of joy and happiness—Do not then, for shame, deface thy nature, nor make thyself unworthy of these celestial gifts; do not deprive thyself of the power and glory God hath allotted thee, for the possession of a few imperfect, vain, and illusory, pleasures.

When thou hast perfected the contemplation of thy God, and considered the extent of those faculties with which thou art endued, thou wilt be fit to receive the following instruction, and to know in thy practice how to conduct thyself.—As thou wilt daily converse with the heavens, so instruct and form thy mind according to the image of divinity. Learn all the ornaments of virtue, and be sufficiently instructed therein. Be humane, courteous, familiar to all, and easy of access. Afflict not the unfortunate with the terrors of a severe fate; in such cases, inform them of their hard fortune with sympathetic concern; direct them to call upon God to divert the judgments impending over them; to summon up all their fortitude, and to endeavour to remove the threatened evil, by a manly exercise of that free-will with which the all-merciful God hath endowed them. Be modest in conversation, and associate with the sober and learned. Covet not riches, but give freely to the poor, both money and judgment. Let no worldly consideration procure an erroneous judgment from thee, or such as may dishonour this sacred science. Love all thy fellow-creatures, and cherish those honest men who cordially embrace this Art. Be sparing in delivering judgment concerning thy king and country, or of the death of thy prince; for I know experimentally that *Reges subjacent legibus stellarus*[*] in arte. Rejoice in the number of thy friends; and avoid litigious suits and controversies. In thy study, be *totus in illis,* that thou mayest be *singles in arte.*[†] Be not extravagant in the desire of learning every science; be not *aliquid tantum in omnibus*[‡]. Be faithful and complacent; betray no one's secrets, I charge thee; never divulge the trust either friend or enemy hath committed to thy faith. Instruct all men to live well; and be a good example thyself. Avoid the fashion of the times, its luxuries, and lasciviousness; but love thy country, and be its friend. Be not dismayed, though evil spoken of; *conscientia praestat mille testibus*[§]..

---

* [kings are subject to the art of the laws of the stars]
† [entirely in them, singular in the art]
‡ [[knowing] a great amount of something in everything].
§ [conscience is excellent with a thousand witnesses].

POETICAL INVOCATION
TO
URANIA

Descend, Urania, with prolific Flame,
And spread the growing Trophies of thy Name;
Disclose to Man a Knowledge of the Skies,
Whose spangling Beauties draw our wondering Eyes.
Instruct young Students in their Care to know,
The starry Influences on all Things below;
Unveil to them the strange mysterious cause
Of those Effects derived from Nature's Laws;
As fiery Meteors, Comets, Lightning, Thunder,
Eclipses, Blazing Stars, at which Men wonder.
The boist'rous rolling of the troubled Sea;
The daily Tides, their sov'reign Regency.
Whirlwinds, and Water-spouts, which pleasing show
The compound Colours of the heav'nly Bow;
With ev'ry occult Virtue and Attraction,
The rise, the growth, decay and putrefaction,
Of all Sublunaries that can be found,
From noble Birth, to Herbs within the Ground.
How Fire and Water, Air and Earth, agree,
When equipois'd, in social Harmony.
That there's a Chain of Concord down descends,
From Heav'n to Earth ; then back to Heav'n ascends.
By Nature shed to sober Men of Sense,
Orion's Bands, Pleiades' sweet Influence;
Shew that the Stars, which trim the heav'nly Spheres,
Are set for Signs, for Seasons, and for Years;
Which Day by Day to Man doth utter Speech,
And Night to Night this sacred Knowledge teach;
That there's a Time for all Things here below:
A Time to reap, to gather in, and sow;
A Time for Birth to Creatures God has giv'n,
A Time to View the great Expanse of Heav'n.
What shall befal us, if we're wise to look,
Is there contain'd, as in a sacred Book;
What moves our Inclinations, what our Wills;

What gives us Health, what subjects us to ills;
What makes one wise; another raving mad;
Another thrifty, yet in rags in clad:
What makes one born a Beggar, and his Fate
Shall be to rise unto a great Estate;
Another, born in very high Degree,
Descend therefrom, to abject Poverty.
What makes us merry, lovers of the Fair;
And others hate to come where'er they are.
What makes some barren, as we daily see,
While others fruitful are inclin'd to be.
What makes one chuse to change a single Life,
Yet grasp much Mis'ry when he takes a Wife;
And why another shall this Path pursue,
And prove that one is not so blest as two.
What makes one travel both by Sea and Land;
While others hate to move from whence they stand.
What makes on labour much for well-earn'd Praise,
While others, undeserving, wear the Bays.
What makes one Army, going forth to fight,
By one much smaller quickly put to Flight.
Is it not plain the starry Influence forces,
Ordain'd by Heav'n to act in constant Courses?
These Truths unshaken stand within this Book,
Therefore, consider o'er the Leaves, and look;
Where Rules enough you'll find to Practice by,
In the pure Science of Astrology.

AN ILLUSTRATION

OF THE CELESTIAL SCIENCE OF

ASTROLOGY

PART THE FIRST

SENSIBLE as I am of the rooted prejudices of the times, against the venerable science of Astrology, and sensible also of the reproach and obloquy that will be levelled against me by men of obstinate and dogmatical principles; I shall nevertheless venture, upon the basis of TRUTH and EXPERIENCE, to make this feeble effort towards restoring a competent knowledge of that comprehensive science, which in all ages of the World was deemed the chief ornament of society, and the distinguishing excellence of enlightened minds. It is therefore to be lamented that the cultivation of it is become obsolete and unfashionable; and that, owing to the violent disturbances at the close of the last century—to the want of recent information on the subject, and to the too refined notions of modern philosophers, its congenial rays have been so long withheld from shedding their divine light upon these kingdoms.

That an Astrology in the Heavens does really exist, and was ordained of God from the beginning of the world, for the immediate information and direction of his creatures here below, is obviously and incontestibly proved from various parts of those sacred Books, which contain the unerring word of God, and the perfect rule of faith for every good and sober Christian.— To revive the gloomy days of superstition, or to impose on the untaught multitude, precepts of ignorance, is no part of the Author's design.—His aim is, to remove the mote from the eyes of prejudiced men; and by just reasoning, and fair argument, founded on the principles of religion and morality, to shew them that God is a God of order, and created nothing in vain;--that he framed the world by number, weight, and measure, and fixed the whole system of heavenly and earthly things upon so perfect and immutable a plan, that the whole doth work harmoniously and sympathetically together, so as to answer all the various purposes for which they were first ordained;—that superiors do uniformly rule inferiors; and that celestial bodies sensibly act upon and influence all earthly substances, whether animal, vegetable, or mineral; not by chance or accident, but by a regular inherent cause, implanted in them from the beginning, by the omnipotence of God.

It is a maxim with persons of a contumacious turn of mind, to consider every thing as impossible, that does not immediately fall within the compass of their own ideas; forgetting that the operations of Nature are as unsearchable as they are curious, and that the ways of God surpass all human comprehension!—and so warped are they from every sentiment of liberality, that those who discover a willingness to receive instruction, or who differ from them in opinion, are condemned to ridicule and scorn. But to shew how reprehensible such conduct is, we need only reflect on the unbelieving St. Thomas, and the pointed exclamation of our Saviour, upon that occasion. Men of this untoward disposition, will take up my book from the impulse of curiosity, 'till recollecting themselves, they will toss it with contempt into some obscure corner, and upbraid its author perhaps in terms not the most liberal or pleasing. And yet, I am bold to say, that even such persons, invulnerable as they may be to the force of reason, might soon be convinced of the purity and excellence of this Science, would they but for a time divest themselves of prejudice, and impartially weigh the evidence brought in its support.—Nay, I have reason to believe, that how much soever they appear externally to condemn Astrology, they nevertheless feel in their own mind, and vainly attempt to stifle, an internal conviction of its absolute existence. Would they but wisely cultivate this internal evidence, and put on the solid reasoning of dispassionate men, the order of nature would then unfold itself to their view, and the stupendous works of Creation captivate their senses; 'till emulous of attaining the most exalted knowledge, they would seek the vast extent of space, and find the whole canopy of heaven expanded for their contemplation. And thus familiarized in the wonderful properties of heavenly and earthly things, they would no longer consider Astrology as the parent of wicked compact and infatuation, or the child of imposture, but would be sensible it contains the balsamic nutriment of Truth and Wisdom.

Those who deny the being of Astrology, have surely never contemplated the mysteries of their own existence, nor the common occurrences that are inseparable from it; many of which are inexplicable when abstractedly considered, and only cease to strike us with wonder, because they are obvious and familiar to our senses. If we recollect that the most trivial incident in nature, cannot come to pass without a cause; and that these causes are incessantly giving birth to a new fate, which at one time brings us comfort, and at another overwhelms us with misfortunes; that to-day gives us the full enjoyment of our wishes, and to-morrow confounds every imagination of our hearts; it is strange we should deny that such causes exist, when every hour's experience confirms the fact, by the good or ill success that constantly attends all human pursuits. To illustrate this observation more fully, let us attentively consider the stupendous frame or model of Nature, as laid down in the holy Scriptures, and endeavour to deduce therefrom the subordinate dependence of one part upon another, from the interior heavens, to the minutest substance upon earth. Hence we may possibly discover the origin of these causes, and prove that Astrology does not exist in imagination only.

The substance of this great and glorious Frame, which, the Almighty created, we call the world; and the world consists of the heaven and the earth *. The model of it is, as the prophet Ezekiel describes it, in the form of a wheel † with many wheels within the same, involved one within another. And thus we find it by mathematical demonstration; for the earth is a wheel or globe of sea and land, circumscribed by the atmosphere, as within a greater wheel, which is globous too; and surrounded by the heavens, as by many wheels involved one within another, encircling the sun, moon, and stars, and all the host of them. The power which first actuated and put these wheels in perpetual motion, was the same which called them into existence; the executioners of whose will, are represented by the Prophet under the similitude of four living' creatures, immeasurably endued with wisdom, courage, agility, and strength. And hence were life, and spirit, and power, and virtue communicated to the heavens, and from the heavens to the earth, and from the earth to man and beast, and to every plant and herb, and earthly substance. Hence also are derived the magnetic powers, and wonderful properties of nature; the virtues of sympathy and antipathy, the invisible effects of attraction and expulsion, and all the various influences of the stars and planets.

The proper agents of this noble structure, are angels, and men; the one composed of a pure etherial spirit, and incorruptible; the other, in his primary state, less pure, but incorruptible also, until his fall, which brought

* See Gen. i. 1,
† Ezek. i. 15. 16,

upon himself and offspring mortality and death. The angels are either good or bad, and ultimately know their reward or doom; but the works of fallen man are yet upon the anvil, and time with us is still going on. But man is now endued, as in his primary state, with the agency of a Free Will, and hath good and evil, for a test of his obedience, continually set before him, with freedom to choose either. And thus, unconstrained either by the immediate hand of God, or by the operation of the planets, as second causes, some embrace life, and others seek condemnation; and hence follow virtue and vice, prosperity and adversity, sickness and health, life and death, and all the vicissitudes of Fortune. And though the rise and fall of empires proceed from the virtues and vices of those men who govern and inhabit them; and these virtues and vices proceed from the free will or agency of those men; and though the incidents good and bad of one man's life are innumerable, and the men who are the subjects of those incidents in one single age, are innumerable also; and though the ages of men, since the creation of the world, are innumerable too; yet have all these multiplied incidents, whether trivial or important, come to pass by a regular course or concatenation of causes, originally implanted in the wheels or frame of nature. And with such minute perfection was this stupendous frame constructed, that neither the fall of man, nor the tremendous shock which agitated the world upon that afflicting occasion; not all the wickedness of mankind in after ages, nor the desolations which have rent the earth in consequence thereof, have yet impaired the wheels of this astonishing machine, or for a moment impeded its constant and unceasing motion. And such was the amazing foresight and providence of God, that perceiving, at one view, all the events of futurity, the turnings and windings of every man's will, and the total sum and upshot of all virtue and vice, he at once contrived the fates of prosperity and adversity, of rewards and punishments so to come up, as precisely to answer the virtues and prayers of the righteous, and the vices and profaneness of the wicked, in all ages of the world, at their fit and appointed seasons.

Now all mankind have each of them, more or less, a certain share of wisdom, power, or wealth, wherewith they occupy in this life, and carry forward all their undertakings. Thus we see some men, by means of riches, courage or contrivance, grow mighty, and purpose, as if nothing could impede the full accomplishment of their designs; and yet we find there are two things which confound the wisest, the greatest, and proudest of them all, in the very summit of their glory;——these are, Time, and Chance—two mighty lords upon earth, which bring to pass many strange and marvellous events. Time is that motion of space which proceeded out of eternity when the world began, and holdeth us unto eternity, which is to succeed at the world's end. Out of this one long time, are engendered infinite spaces of time, of a great variety of sort; and these are either general or special, and each of them either fortunate, or unfortunate. There is a time for every purpose under heaven *; a time of pleasure, and another time of pain and grief; a time to rise, and a time to fall; a time to be born, and a time to die. There is a certain lucky time in man's life, wherein if he go out to battle, though with but few men, yet he carrieth the victory; and there is another time wherein, though he go out with ever so complete an army, yet shall he gain nothing but disgrace † So also there is a time when overtures of marriage shall be successful, but a man's desires answer it not, and again there is a time when desires of marriage shall strongly urge, and all overtures prove ineffectual; but there is a time also when desires and overtures shall exactly correspond, and suit together. In like manner, there is a time when prosperity and riches shall offer themselves, and be attained, whether a man sleep or wake; and by and by, though he pursue them with wings, yet so unlucky a time occurs, as renders all his endeavours fruitless. Some men come into the world in a lucky hour, so that let them be wise or foolish, they shall be buoyed up on the wings of fate in all matters of wealth or honour, and succeed in all that they take to; while wiser and better men, smitten with an unlucky time of birth, shall be as undeservedly disparaged, and all their undertakings shall prove unsuccessful and unhappy. Some shall be lucky in the van of their enterprises, and as unfortunate in the rear; and others again contrariwise. And thus time seems to mock and sport with the men of this life, and to advance, or counteract, all their skill and contrivances, even to a degree infinitely beyond whatever we could reasonably conceive or expect. And yet time of itself is but a dead thing, and a mere instrument; but the wheels of the heavens turning upon it, imprint riddles in its face, and carve and cut out the various shapes of prosperity and adversity, upon the minutest portion thereof. And wonderful it is to observe, that a child, the moment it draws breath, becomes time-smitten by the face of heaven, and receives an impression from the stars therein, which taking rise from the ascendent, sun, moon, and other principal significators, operate as the impressors stand, and point out, as with the finger of God, the causes whence the <u>fate and fortune of the newborn infant proceed; and whether it come</u>

* See Eccl. iii. 1, 2, &c.
† Chap. ix. 11.

before, or at its full time, or in what part of the world soever it is born, it matters not; for as the nature of the significators are that ascend upon the horizon at the birth, such shall certainly be the fortune of the* native. This is a truth that will bear the most minute enquiry, and will be found the ordination of an all-wise and indulgent Providence, for the speculation and improvement of his creature man. And these significators represent, as it were, a series of curious knots, which untie by course; and as every knot unties, different times seem to fly out, and perform their errands; and of these, sometimes we may observe two, or three, or more, lucky knots opening together, and at other times as many that are inauspicious. Yet *all times are beautiful in their seasons*, if men could hit them; but through the malignity of sin, and an intemperate pursuit of worldly pleasures, we often lose the favourable time afforded us, of embracing the most substantial happiness.

The second great lord over human inventions, is Chance. And these chances proceed from a great variety of rare and secret operations of heaven, which throw in the way of men those strange and fortuitous turns of fortune, that surpass all human foresight or conception. And yet there is really no such thing as chance in nature; much less can there be any thing that comes by chance, in respect of God; but all those curious hits that strike in between the cause and its effect, we call Chances, as best suiting human ideas, because of the undescribable properties of them. For in shuffling a pack of cards, or in casting the dice, it seems to us a meer chance what cast shall happen uppermost, or what card will go to the bottom of the pack, and yet it is evident by experience, that there is a certain luck in nature, which presides over all these adventures, so that a man shall either win or lose in a methodical course. It also happens in the time of battle, and in every pursuit after wealth and honor, that chances fall in upon us, and turn the scales by a secret kind of fate, beyond all that could reasonably have been expected; and thus heaven breathes into all human actions, an infinity of these chances, that overturn the wisdom and power, and all the greatness of man. These chances are uniformly managed by a certain kind of luck, either good or bad, which drives the nail; and this,

---

*This astonishing property of nature will be illustrated more at large, in its proper place, and the reader enabled, by plain and obvious rules, to make the experiment upon himself, upon his own family, or upon any other subjects he may think proper.—The event of his own observations will confirm the fact, and afford him an inexhaustible fund of moral and religious contemplation!

by some heavenly influence, that infuses a secret virtue or poison into our actions, as courage into their hearts on one side, or dismay on the other; and skill into some mens heads to pursue the right course to be rich, or folly into others, whereby they run headlong to misery and want; or else fortunateth or infortunateth by mistake of words, signals, or acts, that turn to the best or worst advantage, by strange hits or miscarriages; and thus it happens that a slight mistake in battle begets an utter rout, after a victory made almost complete, by the meer utterance of a wrong word, or steering an improper course. But which way soever it happens, the whole matter is wrought by a good or ill luck, and the hand of God is at the bottom of it; not by any new contrived act, but by the same , regular course of nature, ordained from the beginning of the world.

Thus both Time and Chance are the servants of nature, under whose commands they sway the world, and worldly men; but by her laws are both of them disposed. Time measures out the extent of mens lives, and sets bounds how long they may live by strength of nature, and how much of that time shall be extenuated by means of sin; and it also carves out limits to the particular fates of all mankind; and Chance acts in observance of those limits, and brings about the good and bad success of every fate. And thus by the service of Time and Chance, nature performs all her great and secret operations, whether upon collective bodies, or places, or persons. It may be thought strange that nature should bring forth men and women at a great distance of years, hours, and places, all destined to die at one time, and by the same manner of death, either by war, plague pestilence, or shipwreck; and that time and chance should pick them up, and draw them together, from a variety of different pursuits, to partake at last in one and the same destructive fate. Yet this is no more strange than true; for these things frequently happen, and that by the imperceptible influences of those heavenly aspects and stars, which *in their courses fought against Sisera*[*]. And by the same rule, as many men, women, and children, are, on the other hand, gathered together by a similar force and virtue, to enjoy great and good fortune.

Some perhaps will contend, that these operations of nature are incompatible with the free agency of man's will. But if what has already been premised be attentively considered, this supposition will immediately vanish; for God, who ordained the course of nature, certainly foresaw the minutest turn of every man's will, and eventually contrived his fate to correspond therewith, so as to admit its free and uncontrouled choice.

[*] Judg, v, 20.

And whoever denies this antecedent principle, or prescience of God in the construction of the world, denies one of his most essential attributes. The Will of man, without doubt, in a variety of instances, makes great struggles and wrestlings with the starry influences, both in good and in evil pursuits, and often prevails over them exceedingly;— for though a person be born under such benevolent or malignant aspects, as shall point out his natural temper and disposition, and indicate the principal transactions, fortunate or unfortunate, that are likely to be the distinguishing marks of his life; yet does it depend entirely upon the free uncontrouled will of that man, whether all those circumstances, so pointed out in his nativity, shall come to pass, or not; because the free will in every man, when fortified by habits of virtue and wisdom, often enable him to over-rule those evil aspects, so as to avoid the commission of any criminal offence, and to guard him against the misfortunes or losses impending over him; while men of a profligate and careless habit, not only lose the advantages of a promising nativity, but, if born under malevolent aspects, are often reduced to the last stage of distress, and perish under the very same strokes of nature, which wiser and better men, born in the same inauspicious moments, have endured with much ease. And thus far *sapiens dominabitur astris*, the wise man, above the fool, may rule his stars. But we must not forget, that under these operations of fate, there are many influences so powerful, that no wisdom of man can oppose. Such are the fatal wounds of death, when nature's glass is run out, and such the violent blows of excruciating, pain and sickness, and the high tides of prosperity and adversity; in all which cases, we find by experience, *astra regunt homines*, the stars rule, and overpower men. Yet nevertheless, such is the infinite prescience and providence of God, that foreseeing the desires and deserts of all wise and holy men, in their different ages and times, he also laid their fates suiting to their actions. He foresaw Joseph's prayers and tears in his captivity, and accordingly provided his advance in nature to correspond therewith[*]. He foresaw Hannah's falling, and earned: prayer, and ordained her opening womb to bud forth in course of nature exactly answering thereto [†]. So that the wisdom and will of man has its full free work, without restraint or controul; and grace and virtue act by their own principles, as they are led by the Holy Ghost; and yet nature, as it was contrived from all eternity, acts freely too. This is the doctrine we are taught by the word of God, which is confirmed by the evidence of our own reason and experience.

[*] Sec Gen. xxxvir. and xli. 40. Pfal. cv. 1S, 19, 20.
[†]—Sam. i. 10, n, &c.

Now the science which we call Astrology, is nothing more than the study or investigation of this frame or model of nature, with all its admirable productions and effects; whereby we acquire a knowledge of the secret virtues of the heavens, and the shining luminaries therein contained. It is a science which all may attain to, by common diligence and application; and the more we delight in it, the more readily do we foresee the motions of future events, and the curiosities of chance and natural accidents, and the courses of luck by which both are governed, and the order of fate, unto which all of them are subservient; together with all the most curious act of attracting and expelling, alluring and threatening, encouraging and disheartening, and all such like operations of nature, most secretly and imperceptibly performed, beyond the reach of imagination. And as by a skill in this study we attain to see and experience things that are past, so by the same skill we attain to a knowledge of things which are to come and, by knowing the time of our birth, are enabled to read in the heavens the story of our whole lives, our blessings and crosses, honour and dishonour, prosperity and adversity, sickness and health, and all the years of our life, and time of our death, even as though we had seen them transacted and come to pass in their several times and seasons. For God hath assuredly given this knowledge unto the wise man, *to know the time and the judgment, and the number of our days, that we may be certified how long we have to 'live*, with comfort and content; that we may be timely prepared for all states of prosperity and adversity, for a long and happy life, or a calamitous and speedy death; and that we may support ourselves with fortitude and resignation, in proportion to our foreknowledge of these events. And no man so fit to foreknow these, as he who is able to say, *Major sum quam cui possit fortuna nocere*[†].

But many men will not believe, that by natural means all or any of this foreknowledge can be fairly and lawfully obtained; or that the influences attributed to the heavenly bodies have any foundation in truth. It is therefore necessary, before I enter upon the practical part of the science, to bring such evidence in support of what has been already advanced, as will be found incontrovertible and decisive; and for this purpose I must refer to the testimony of those sacred writings, which contain the revelation of God, and in which the doctrine of this science is so demonstrably proved, that it will be difficult to believe the one, without admitting the other. Let us consider the account given by Moses,

---

* Ecd. i. 5. Pfah xxxix. 4, 5.
†[I am too great for Fortune to harm me. From Ovid Metamorphoses 6: 195]

of the creation of the heavenly bodies. God said, "Let there be lights in the firmament of heaven, to divide the day from the night; the greater light to rule the day, and the lesser light to rule the night, and let them be for signs, and for seasons, and for days and years."—-These then were the purposes for which they were ordained, and irrevocably fixed by their great Creator--—first for lights; for had they not a place in the firmament, or were we deprived of their illuminating rays, we should be instantly overwhelmed with impenetrable darkness. Secondly, they are to divide the day from the night; and this they never cease to do; for when the sun, the greater light, is sunk five degrees below our horizon, we call it night; for then tho moon and stars appear, and shed their lesser light, and darkness in some degree is spread around, and every thing declares it to be the state of night. But when the sun, that glorious fountain of life, light, and motion, begins to touch the eastern verge of the horizon, darkness is dispelled, light begins again to dawn, and the stars which beautifully bespangle our hemisphere, are soon obscured by the full blaze of day; but as days and nights are unequal, and never continue in one stay, these celestial luminaries distinguish their resective reigns. Thirdly, they are for signs—not to brutes, for they have not the faculty of understanding them; nor to angels, for they continually behold the face of God, and obey his will in the government of the heavenly bodies, at his pleasure. Therefore when God faith, *Let them be for signs*, he must speak in reference to man whom he formed a rational creature, capable of distinguishing one sign from another, and of improving by them. Nor are we to look upon them as mere signs, like beacons upon a hill, or as only setting bounds to days, months, and years; but we are to consider them as signs and tokens of those hidden events of futurity, which it concerns every wise and good man to know; and which he may always foresee, by a virtuous and sober study of these intelligent signs, placed by God for that purpose in the firmament of heaven. And that this was the intent of them, is clearly demonstrated by the words of our Saviour, when he foretold the destruction of Jerusalem, and the final consummation of all things. His apostles asked him, What shall the sign of these things be? He replies. Earthquakes, famines, and pestilences; fearful sights in the heavens, and signs in the sun, in the moon and in the * stars. Such also was the sign by which the Eastern Sages discovered the birth of our Saviour, and the place of his nativity; and numerous other instances may be adduced, both from sacred and profane history, in support of this doctrine.-The fourth use of these celestial luminaries, is for seasons. This is also obvious; for we find that heat and

*Luke xxi. 6, 7, u, 25, Sic.

cold, and drought and moisture, are all guided and governed by the heavenly bodies; and that not only spring and autumn, and summer and winter, bear testimony of it; but we have it confirmed by the evidence of our own constitution and feeling; for when the weather is heavy and lowering, we find ourselves dull and languid; when bright and radiant, we are chearful and merry; and, when unsettled and unseasonable, we feel it by indisposition and melancholy; and this is all brought about by the operation of these luminaries upon the seasons of the year, in the due course of nature. The next use allotted them is fifthly for days, and sixthly for years; and that these are measured out, and governed by them, is every way apparent; by the sun's circuit, and the moon's energy.—The sun, like a strong man, rejoices to run his race; he riseth out of the chambers of the east, and with golden rays dispels the morning clouds, and exhales the pearly dew; chearing and refreshing all nature with his presence. Hence it is evident that these luminaries were not only placed in the heavens to give light upon the earth, to govern the seasons, and to set bounds to time; but also to communicate signs and tokens to mankind, of things to come. We shall now consider how far it is scriptural, and consonant to reason, to allow them those influences attributed to them by Astrology.

That the sun, moon, and all the planets, have a direct and obvious influence upon earthly substances, no man of common observation will pretend to deny. The sun is the fountain of heat, and that heat is the nurse of life; and the moon is the fountain of moisture, which tempers the violent heat of the sun, and modifies all his operations. But the sun and moon, and all the planets, have each of them a particular specific property, according to their own innate quality, and according to the nature of that sign or band of stars under which they happen to be posited. This is a fact established by repeated observation and experience; for when the sun enters the equinoctial sign Aries, the spring begins to shew herself, and all vegetative nature, by the moon's humidity and the sun's temperate heat, seems to revive and flourish, and, as it were, to rise from the dead; whither the cold blasts of the hyemnal air, had before consigned it.- So, when his radiant beams enter the sign Taurus, they stir up the benign influences of the Pleiades and Hyades; Hoedi being, then to the north, and Orion to the south, and Arcturus sinking below the horizon; and their cold and tempestuous effects begin to cease, as they are succeeded by these benevolent constellations which produce warm southern winds, and gentle showers, replenishing the earth, and causing vegetation. Again, when the sun rises with the Dog-star, we find an influence which causes vehemency of heat, contagion, and infirmity. Medicaments administered under this constellation, prove hard and obnoxious; and we find dogs at this time are apt to run mad; the sea is troubled without any apparent cause, and all nature seems more or less oppressed by it; and yet these effects are never found to be equally violent in any two summers, which clearly proves an influence in the stars, as well as in the sun. And again, though the sun, keeps the same constant and invariable course through the twelve signs of the Zodiac, for an infinity of annual revolutions, yet we never find the seasons and weather exactly correspond, which they doubtless would do, were it not that cold and heat, and wind and rain, are governed by the configurations the sun has with the planets and fixed stars; and this also evidently proves the force of their influence. It is likewise manifest, that, whenever the planet Saturn is passing out of one sign into another, the weather, is more or less turbulent and unsettled.

But it is not the weather only, nor the inanimate part of the creation alone, that is affected by the influences of the sun, moon, and planets; for we find they operate upon the human species, and upon all animate nature, in every part of the world. The sun, and the quality of the heavens about the torrid zone, naturally occasion those men who are born and live under it to be quite black, with short crisped hair, of a mean, stature, and hot constitution, imbibing a fierce and savage spirit; and this by reason of the sun's continual stay and power in that fiery regions. It is observable, that the inhabitants of the south, are of a better an quicker wit, and much more ingenious and tractable; and this is accounted for by their vertical point being situated nearer the zodiac, in which the planet moves. So likewise the inhabitants of the north are of a strong body, but of rude manners and condition, because their vertical point is placed at a great distance from the sun's course; and therefore they abound with cold and moisture, and are of a phlegmatic constitution, of a fair complexion, tall, courageous, and ingenuous. Europe, being situated in the north-west part of the earth, is under Mars in Aries; and, by reason of this planet ruling in that triplicity, its inhabitants are naturally of a noble and magnanimous spirit, given to martial exploits, and feats of war; of a generous mind, and courteous manners. And thus the sun, modified by the different signs and constellations through which he passes, regulates the climates, and sheds his influence upon all mankind, leaving behind him evident marks of his government and sway. Some, indeed, have attempted to account for the swarthy and black complexion of the savage race, by a variety of other plausible conjectures; but none are to be relied on, that do not attribute its cause to the intense heat and power of the sun in those climates; than which nothing can be more consonant to reason, since we find, even in this country, that if we remain long together in the sun, in the heat of summer, our complexions change, and we become in a degree tanned and swarthy.

Conspicuous as are the influences of the sun, those of the moon are no less so. This is evinced by a consideration of that wonderful and never ceasing operation of the moon upon the ocean, so as to occasion that perpetual flux and reflux of the sea, which we call tides. Here we see the waters of the vast ocean, forgetful, as it were, of their natural rest, move and roll in tides obsequious to the strong attractive power of the moon, and with an increase or diminution of force, in proportion as she appears in strength, or want of aspect. This is an influence so universally admitted, and so peculiar to that luminary, that it establishes at once the doctrine we contend for. But there are numerous other instances of the effects of the moon, no less common than extraordinary, and perfectly well known. Those unhappy persons who labour under a deprivation of sense, and are afflicted with lunacy, have their fits more violent and terrible, in proportion as the moon increases or diminishes in light and motion; and, in all chronic and acute diseases, her power and influence are visibly and forcibly felt. Indeed every subject of the creation is more or less effected by the moon's energy; the eyes of cats are observed to swell or fall at the full and change of the moon; and even the shell-fish at the bottom of the ocean, are known to feel the weight of her influence. Those who sleep in the fields, or in any place exposed to the open air, by moon-light, find their heads oppressed with water, and their senses inert and heavy; and butcher's meat hung up, and exposed to the moon-light, will soon putrify. The gardener also brings us abundant testimonies of the influence of the moon upon the vegetable world. If pease are sown in the increase of the moon, they never cease blooming; and, if fruits and herbs are set in the wane, experience shews they are neither so rich in flavour, nor so strong and healthy, as when planted during her increase; so vines, because they should not spread too fast, are usually pruned in the wane. It is also remarkable that a pomegranate will live only as many years as the moon was days old when it was planted; and, in planting shrubs, or the like, if they are to shoot up strait and tall, and to take little root, they are set when the moon is in an airy sign and increasing in light; but contrariwise when they are to take deep root, and to strike downwards. And thus we may observe flowers that are under the moon's influence only open their blossoms in the-night; whilst those which are peculiarly under the government of the sun open every morning when he begins to rise, and close in the evening when he sinks below the horizon. These effects and influences of the moon are so common, and so generally known, that it were almost needless to repeat them here, but for the purpose of drawing this conclusion, that, as one planet has a known and forcible action upon sublunary things, it is natural to believe that all the others are endued in some degree with a similar force and virtue. Indeed most physicians know that the planet Saturn rules all climacterical years, as the sun doth critical days, and the moon the crisis of all acute diseases; and that every seventh year Saturn comes to the square or opposition of his place in the radix of every man's nativity; and that, after the revolution of the sun, he becomes the chief ruler of critical days, and is often observed, by his configurations with the moon, to set aside the fatal crisis of those desperate disorders, over which the patient was not expected to live. From these physical reasons, we may safely conclude that Saturn is by nature cold and melancholy, as the sun is hot and chearful; and, being thus opposite to the sun in quality and effect, so is he in relation to the signs and mansions of the heavens where he bears rule, and therefore inclines always to cold, as the sun does to heat. Hence it follows, that when the sun is in Aquaries, which is the proper sign of Saturn, and opposite to his own sign Leo, the weather inclines more to cold than to heat; and, at every conjunction, square, or opposition, of Saturn with the two great luminaries, we always find the weather cold, moist, and lowering, even in the midst of the summer, unless the rays of Jupiter or Mars interpose, in which case these effects are somewhat less visible. Thus, we may presume to affirm, that the influences of the sun, moon, and planets, are established beyond contradiction.

But, besides these signiorities of the sun, moon, and planets, the *fixed stars* have also their *principalities* in the heavens. The Lord, who gave the sun for a light by day, gave the ordinances of the moon and stars also for a light by night; and to these stars hath he committed a certain *rule* or *dominion*[*] over the day and night, and that promiscuously. Now the stars have no visible operation upon us, besides that little light they administer to our eyes in a dark and clear night; and that is so very small, that all the stars in heaven, besides the sun and moon, are not to be compared, in this

---

*See Jeremiah xxxi. 35. and Gen. i. 18.

respect, with the smallest wax-light; and this little light too is only to be had when the nights are serene and unclouded. Can it then be supposed that God made these glorious bodies, many of which are bigger than the whole earth, and move in their orbs as so many other worlds in the heavens, merely for a twinkle in the night, and that only when the weather permits? lo! every little daisy that grows upon the cold ground has a secret and insensible virtue wrapt in its leaves and flowers; and have these celestial bodies no *influences* but what we now and then catch with our eyes, as they occasionally sparkle their dim glances upon us ? Yes, they have each of them a secret power and virtue, wherewith they act upon all earthly things, as well by day as by night, and in cloudy as well as in clear weather. But, as their operations are not performed by sensible and palpable means, it follows that they have a secret and hidden way of rule, whereby the influences are imperceptibly infused into every concern of this life. And, as have the stars, so also have the sun and moon, a secret and imperceptible action, peculiar to themselves; for it is not the mere heat that gives life, nor the mere moisture that sustains it; for, if that were the case, then might man make living creatures artificially. It is true that heat may hatch the eggs, but all the ingenuity of man cannot make an egg that can be hatched; for there is a secret operation of the sun and moon, independent of heat and moisture, necessary to the production of life, both in vegetive and sensitive animals. And in these secret and insensible operations, besides the *light* that they give, consists that *rule* which the sun, moon, and stars, were ordained to exercise over all the sons of day and night; and herein are written all those *ordinances* of the moon and stars, which are to be a *law* unto mankind, and to the whole body of nature, so long as the world * endures. Thus the stars have their natural influences, assigned to them in the frame of nature, from the beginning of the world; and these influences are diffused upon all earthly things, as far as day and night extend their limits. And this God himself confirms when he says to Job, " Canst thou bind the sweet *influences of Pleiades*, or loose the bands of Orion ?—Canst thou bring forth Mazzaroth in his season; or canst thou *guide* Arcturus with his sons?"† Whence it is evident that the stars called the Pleiades have their *ordinances*, that is, their *sweet influences*, which no power of man is able to restrain. And the stars of Orion have their *ordinances*, and binding faculty, by showers in summer, and frost in winter, bringing such an hard and tough coat of armour upon the ground, as all the contrivances of man are not able to prevent. Thus

* Jeremiah xxxi. 35, 36.
† Job xxxviii

Mazzaroth, and Arcturus with his sons,* have also their ordinances, and the whole host of heaven have their course, by which the purposes of God, and all the events of this life, are uniformly brought to pass.

---

* See Argol. aftr. ante Ephem lib. ii cap. 8 Stellae tempestuosae sunt Orion, Arcturus,&c. pluriosae Pleiades.

A Summary VIEW of the WORKS of CREATION in the CONSTRUCTION of NATURE

NATURE is that which God has ordained Empress over all the Works of his Creation, and over every part of the Celestial and Terrestrial World. This world comprehends both the Heaven and the Earth, and is compounded of three separate and distinct parts, which are also called Worlds, namely, an Elementary world, which is the lowest in dignity; a Celestial world, which is next above the elementary; and an Etherial world, which is the highest of all; and these three less worlds, make the one entire Great World. In the order of Nature, the all-wise and supreme Being has ordained that every inferior should be governed by its superior; and by this eternal decree, the Intellectual world actuates and governs the Celestial, which consists of the sun, moon, and stars, and all the host of heaven; and the Celestial world actuates and governs the Elementary world, and all elementary bodies, whether animal, mineral, or vegetable.

The Elementary world is composed of the four elements, Fire, Air, Earth, and Water, of which all things peculiar to the elementary world are generated; but these elements, in the state we commonly find them, are not pure, but intermixed with each other; and they often change one into the other by nature, as fire turns into smoke, and smoke into air, and air into water, &c. Each of these elements has likewise two specific qualities, viz. fire is hot and dry, water is cold and moist, air is hot and moist, and the earth is cold and dry; so that fire is inimical to water, and air to earth. These elements also possess three essential properties inherent in themselves, viz. air has motion, thinness, and darkness; fire has motion, brightness, and thinness; water has motion, darkness, and thickness; and earth has darkness, thickness, and quietness; so that fire is twice more thin than air, thrice more moveable, and four times more bright; air is twice more bright, three times more thin, and four times more moveable, than water; water is twice more bright, thrice more thin, and four times more moveable, than earth; as therefore fire is to air, so is air to water, and water to earth; and *vice versa*, as earth is to water, so is water to air, and air to fire. Three of these elements have motion, and are active; but the earth is fixed and passive, and only supplies matter for the other elements to act upon; for as nothing can be produced unless matter be subministered, so of necessity one element must subminister that matter for the operation of the others: and no influence could be dispensed by the heavens, unless there were elementary bodies to receive their influence; therefore every active principle must of necessity be in motion, and every passive principle must be at rest. And accordingly, as the active elements find the earth that they act upon to be pure, or impure, so will the work be that is produced. The earth can bring forth nothing of itself, but is the womb or matrix into which the other elements distil or project their seminal virtues; and in proportion as it is impregnated by their force and energy, it brings forth, according to the due course of nature. The Earth also receives the celestial rays and influences of all the heavenly bodies, as ordained by God, to be the object, subject, and receptacle of them; whereby it not only brings forth what is intended to be produced, but also multiplies what it receives, and separates the good from the bad, and the pure from the impure. It likewise contains the seeds or seminal virtues of all elementary bodies, and hath a triplicity in itself, viz. mineral, animal, and vegetive. It is the common fountain or mother from whence all things spring, whose fruitfulness is produced by the three-fold operation of fire, air, and water. And, as these elementary bodies possess most extraordinary qualities, it will be proper to consider each of them distinctly, and to explain their several properties more at large.

Fire, the first active element, is an elastic body, composed of infinitely small particles, scarcely, if at all, adhering to each other, and a body in motion. It is in effect, the universal instrument of all the motion and action in the universe; without fire, all bodies would become immoveable, as in a severe winter we actually see our fluids become solid for want of it. Without fire a man would harden into a statue, and the very air would cohere into a firm rigid mass. Fire then is the sole cause of all mutation or change; for all mutation is by motion, and all motion by fire. Upon the absence of only a certain degree of fire, all oils, fats, waters, wines, ales, spirits of wine, vegetables, and animals, become, hard, rigid, and inert; and the less the degree of fire, the sooner is this induration made. Hence, if there were the greatest degree of cold, and all fire was absolutely taken away, all nature would grow into one concrete body, solid as gold, and hard as diamond; but upon the re-application of fire, it would recover its former mobility. So that upon this one element of fire, depends all fluidity of humours and juices; also all vegetation, putrefaction, fermentation, animal heat, and a thousand other things. Fire is in itself but one, though it centers in divers places. It centers in the heavens, and is boundless, where it guards and preserves nature, and enlivens all the creation, giving life, light, and motion, to all creatures, and stirs them up to fecundity and fruitfulness. It centers also in the earth, where it generates metals, minerals, and stones; and, by joining itself with the beams of the celestial sun and moon, produces vegetation upon the surface of the earth. It occasions that heat we sometimes observe in springs and fountains; and imparts a principle of its own into whatever it produces, so that whatsoever retains life retains it by virtue of its own inclosed heat; and, whenever this is exhausted or extinguished, it perishes and dies. And, as water purgeth, cleanseth, and dissolveth, all things that are not fixed, so fire purgeth and perfecteth all things that are fixed; and, as water conjoins all things that are dissolved, so fire separates all things that are conjoined; it causes all seeds to grow and ripen; and, when they are ripe, it expels them by the sperm into divers places of the earth; and, as the situation and temperature of these places are, whether hot or cold, moist or dry, pure or impure, so will the diversity of things be both in the bowels, and upon the surface of the earth. But, amongst all the wonderful properties of fire, there are none more extraordinary than this; That, though it is the principal cause of almost all the sensible effects that continually fall under our observation, yet it is in itself of so infinitely a subtle nature, that it baffles or defeats our most sagacious enquiries, nor ever comes within the cognizance of our senses.

Fire may be divided into three kinds or species, viz. celestial, subterraneous, and culinary. Celestial fire is that which is peculiar to the celestial regions, where it exists in the greatest purity and perfection, unmixed with smoke, or any of that gross, feculent, or terrestrial matter, found in culinary and subterranean fire; but allowing for this difference, the effects of the celestial fire appear to be the same as those of the culinary. Subterraneous fire is that which manifests itself in fiery eruptions of the earth, volcanoes, or burning mountains, and is always found in the more central parts of the earth, and often in mines and coal-pits. Culinary fire is that which we employ in all chemical operations, and in the common occasions of life. To ascertain the force and power of fire, the learned Boerhaave made innumerable curious experiments, which enabled him to divide it into six degrees. The first degree is that by which nature performs the office of vegetation in plants, and by which chemistry imitates and does the like. This commences from the highest degree of cold, which in Fahrenheit's thermometer is denoted by one; and ends at eighty degrees, since in this whole interval vegetables of one kind or other give indication of life and growth; so that if all plants be examined by the degrees of heat contained within these limits, we shall find all of them come to maturity in one or other of these intermediate degrees. This heat is suited to extracting the native spirits of odoriferous vegetables with oils, as that of roses, jessamin, and the like. Thus the fragrant scent of roses may be communicated to oil, by putting the inodorous and insipid oil of olives in a tall clean chemical glass, and digesting it in a heat of fifty-six degrees, with the most fragrant roses, gathered just as they are opening in a morning; the application of a similar degree of heat would also impregnate alcohol with the purest spirit of saffron. The second degree of fire may be accounted that of the human body in a healthy state. This degree is always greater than that of the ambient air, and may be supposed to commence at the 40th degree of the thermometer, and end about the 94th. Within this compass animals may live and subsist, that is, if their juices be of any degree of heat within these bounds. The eggs of insects subsist unhurt during hard winters, and hatch in the succeeding spring. Fishes, both of the sea and of rivers, live in water which is only thirty-four degrees warm; and fishes that have lungs, and all respiring animals in a state of health, communicate to their humours a warmth of ninety-two degrees; and therefore the utmost limits of this degree are fixed at thirty-three and ninety-four. Within the compass of this heat are included the vital actions of animals; the fermentation of vegetables, and the putrefaction both of vegetables and animals; and likewise the generation, breeding, hatching, birth, and nutrition, of animals. This degree is also employed by chemists to prepare elixirs, volatile alkaline salts, and tinctures. The third degree of fire is that which extends from ninety-four degrees of the thermometer to 212; at which, last, water usually boils. This degree is required in the distillation of simple and compound waters, the essential oils of vegetables; and will coagulate or consolidate the serum, blood, and other animal juices, and consequently destroy life. The fourth degree of heat may by reckoned from the degree 212 to 600; within which limits all oils, saline lixivia, mercury, and oil of vitriol, are distilled; lead and tin will also melt and mix together. The oils, salts, and saponaceous juices, of animals and vegetables, are rendered volatile and acrid, and become more or less alcalescent; their solid, parts are calcined, and lose their distinguishing qualities and proper virtues; and with this degree of fire, fossil sulphur and sal ammoniac are sublimed. The fifth degree is that wherein the other metals melt, and which commences from six hundred degrees of the thermometer, and ends where iron is held in a state of fusion. In this degree most bodies are destroyed; but glass, gold, silver, copper, and iron, remain long unchanged; all other fixed bodies grow red-hot in this degree, and all the unvitrifiable stones are calcined. The sixth and highest degree of fire hitherto known, is that of the burning lens, or speculum, by M. Villette, Tschirnbaufen, Buffon, and others. The focus of these lenses will even volatilize what is called the metalline or mercurial part of gold, and vitrify the more terrestrial. The utmost degree of fire is the vitrification of fixed bodies, which the ancient magi, or the astrologers of the east, discovered; and they predicted the final end of the world by fire, and its mutation into transparent glass.

Air is the next active element that engages our attention, and it is divided into *proper* or *elementary*, and *common* or *heterogeneous*. Elementary air, properly so called, is a subtile, homogeneous, elastic, matter; the basis or fundamental ingredient of common air, and that which gives it the denomination. It likewise enters into the composition of most or perhaps all bodies, and exists in them under a solid from, deprived of its elasticity, and most of its distinguishing properties, and serving as the cement, and universal bond, of nature; but capable, by certain processes, of being disengaged from them, recovering its elasticity, and resembling the air of our atmosphere. The peculiar nature of this aerial matter we know but little of; what authors have advanced concerning it being chiefly conjectural. We have no way of altogether separating it from the other matter, with which, in its purest state, it is more or less combined, and consequently no way of ascertaining, with satisfactory evidence, its peculiar properties, abstractedly from those of other bodies. Philosophers both ancient and modern maintain, with great plausibility, that it is the same with the pure ether, or that fine, fluid, active, matter, diffused through the whole expanse of the celestial regions, and of the interior heavens; and is supposed to be a body *sui generis*, ingenerable, incorruptible, immutable, present in all places and in all bodies.

Common or heterogeneous air is a coalition of corpuscles of various kinds, which together constitute one common mass, wherein we live and move, and which we are continually receiving and expelling by respiration. The whole assemblage of this makes what we call the *atmosphere*; and where this air or atmosphere ends, there the pure ether is supposed to commence, which is distinguished from air, by its not making any sensible refraction of the rays of light, as air does. This common air, says the ingenious Mr. Boyle, is the most heterogeneous body in the universe; and Boerhaave shews it to be an universal chaos, or *colluvies*, of all kinds of created bodies. Beside the matter of light or fire, which continually flows into it from the heavenly bodies, and probably the magnetic effluvia of the earth, whatever fire can volatilize, is found in the air. Hence the whole fossil kingdom must be found in it; for all of that tribe, as salts, sulphurs, stones, and metals, are convertible into fume, and thus capable of being rendered part of the air. Gold itself, the most fixed of all natural bodies, is found to adhere close to the sulphur in mines; and thus to be raised along with it. Sulphurs also make a considerable ingredient of the air, on account of the many volcanoes, grottos, caverns, and other spiracles, chiefly affording that mineral, dispersed through the globe. All parts of the animal kingdom must also be in the air; for, beside the copious effluvia continually emitted from their bodies, by the vital heat, in the ordinary process of perspiration, by means of which an animal, in the course of its duration, impregnates the air with many times the quantity of its own body; we find that any animal when dead, being exposed to the air, is in a certain time wholly incorporated with it. This fact is proved in a very striking manner, by an extraordinary effect produced by those dead bodies, after they became filled with air, which were unfortunately drowned in the Royal George at Spithead, on the 29th of August, 1782. This ship was heeled on her side for the purpose of some repair, when the water rushed into her lower port-holes, and sunk her almost instantaneously. She went down in fourteen fathom water, and fell upon her side, as was evident from her top-masts, which remained above the water in an inclined direction. A considerable time after this fatal accident, she suddenly righted, and her masts became nearly perpendicular. No one could account for this extraordinary circumstance, till an anonymous writer published the following ingenious and correct solution of it:—" By the muster-roll of this unfortunate ship, it appears that 495 souls perished between her decks; and, as the bodies had no way to escape, they of course remained in that situation. Now all bodies in a state of putrefaction ferment, and this fermentation generates large quantities of air, so that a putrifying carcase, inflated by the generation of air, expands itself to a size far exceeding its original bulk, and becomes lighter than water in a very high degree; and will consequently be pressed upwards towards the surface with a power equal to the weight of a quantity of water adequate in bulk to the inflated carcase; and would rise immediately to the surface in a perpendicular line, if not obstructed in its passage. Now it is obvious that the 495 carcases, which lay between the decks until fermentation and putrefaction commenced, would rise as soon as the generated air rendered them specifically lighter than sea-water: and, as fermentation increased their bulk, they would, by their expansion, remove a quantity of water from between the decks, on the lowed side of the ship (to which by their gravity they would naturally incline when their breath first left them), equal to their encreased bulk; and, being then acted upon by the upward pressure of the water, would exert against the under-part of the decks, immediately over them, a power likewise equal to such weight of water as equals their increased bulk. The heaviest tide of the ship, being thus first lightened by the displacing so large a quantity of water, and exchanging it for air; and then acted upon by the pressure of the water upwards against the under side of the inflated carcases, lifting hard against the decks on or beneath the center of the ship; and farther by the pressure of the water upwards, against the underside of the hulls, masts, &c. together with the counterpoise of a large weight of water between decks, on the highest side, would cause her to be nearly in equilibrio; and consequently, the first strong tide (as was the case) would swing her on her keel, and right her."

As to vegetables, none of that class can be wanting in the contribution of their effluvia to the common air, since we know that all vegetables, by putrefaction, become volatile. The associations, reparations, attritions, dissolutions, and other operations, of one sort of matter upon another, may likewise be considered as sources of numerous other neutral or anonymous bodies, unknown to the most inquisitive naturalist. Thus air is one of the most considerable and universal agents in all nature, being concerned in the preservation of life, and the production of most of the phenomena relating to this world. Its properties and effects, including a great part of the researches and discoveries of the modern philosophers, have in a considerable degree been reduced to precise laws and demonstrations; in which form they make a very extensive and important branch of the mixed mathematics, called Pneumatics; for a more perfect knowledge of which, I beg leave to recommend the curious reader to Dr. Priestley's invaluable Experiments and Observations on different kinds of air. But I shall just observe further, that to the pressure of air we are to attribute the coherence of the parts of bodies. Breathing too, on which depends animal life, is owing to the pressure and spring of the air; and to the same cause may be attributed the production of fire and flame, as appears from the sudden extinction of fire when deprived of air. It is likewise necessary for the existence and propagation of sounds, for the germination and growth of plants, for conveying all the variety of smells, and for receiving and transmitting the rays and influences of the celestial world to the terrestrial. Air acts upon all bodies by its common properties of weight and elasticity, and by the peculiar virtues of the ingredients whereof it is composed. These properties of weight and elasticity in the air, when engendered in large quantities in the bowels of the earth, and heated by the subterrancan fire, occasion earthquakes, and other vehement commotions of nature. And by some late experiments of M. de la Hire, it is found that a certain quantity of condensed air, if heated to a degree equal to that of boiling water, would produce an explosion sufficient to tear asunder the solid globe. By means of a corroding acid, air dissolves iron and copper, unless well defended by oil; even gold in the chemist's laboratory, when the air is impregnated with the effluvia of aqua regia, contracts a rust like other bodies. It fixes volatile bodies, and volatilizes those which are fixed. From the different effluviae diffused through the air proceed a variety of effects. Near mines of copper, it will discolour silver and brass; and in London, where the air abounds with acid and corrosive particles, metalline utensils rust much sooner than in the country. Stones also undergo the changes incident to metals. Thus Purbeck stone, of which Salisbury cathedral is built, is observed to become gradually softer, and to moulder away in the air; and Mr. Boyle gives the same account of Blackington stone. It is very difficult to obtain oil of sulphur in a clear dry air, as its parts are then more ready to evaporate; but in a moist cloudy air it may be obtained in abundance. All salts melt most readily in cloudy weather; and reparations proceed best in the same state of the air. If pure wine be carried into a place where the air is full of the fumes of wine then fermenting, it will begin to ferment a-fresh. The wholesomeness and unwholesomeness of air is certainly owing to the different effluvia with which it abounds. The best air is to be found in open champaign countries, where the soil is dry, and spontaneously produces wild thyme, wild marjoram, and the like sweet-scented plants. The morning air is more refreshing than that of the evening, and air agitated with breezes than that which is serene and still. As good air contributes greatly to health, so that which is bad or infectious is no less prejudicial to it, as is evident in contagious diseases, plagues, murrains, and other mortalities, which are spread by an infected air. But this infected air may be corrected, and the body preserved from its fatal effects, by the effluvia of aromatic and strong-scented herbs and flowers. From observations on bleeding in rheumatisms, and after taking cold, it is evident the air can enter with all its qualities, and vitiate the whole texture of the blood, and other juices. From palsies, vertigoes, and other nervous affections, caused by damps, mines, &c. it is evident that air thus qualified, can relax and obstruct the whole nervous system. And from the cholics, fluxes, coughs, and consumptions, produced by damp, moist, and nitrous, air, it is evident it can corrupt and spoil the noble organs of the whole human structure. Thus air is an instrument which nature is universally applying in all her works, consequently a knowledge of its properties seems highly necessary not only to the chemist and physician, but to the philosopher and divine.-For more on this important subject see Hales's Veget. Stat. ch. vi. Sir Isaac Newton's Optics, Qu. 31. p. 371, 372. Buffon's Hist. Nat. Supp. vol. i. M. de la Hire, Mem. de l'Acad. An. 1703. Phil. Trans. vol. lvi. p. 152, &c. Bacon, Nov. Organ, lib. ii. app. 13. Lavoisier's Physical and Chemical Essays, vol. i. Black's Eff. and Obf. Phys. and Liter., vol. ii. Chamb. Cyclop. new Edit. Art. Air. And Priestley on Air.

Water, the third active element, is the menstruum of the world, and is of two kinds; first, Pure Water, which is a limpid and colourness liquor, without smell or taste, simple and volatile, and is peculiar to the celestial regions. Secondly, Gross Water, which is a pellucid fluid, convertible into ice by cold, naturally pervading the strata of the earth, and flowing on its surface, and with the body of the earth constitutes the terraqueous globe. The figure of the component parts of water appears to be smooth and spherical, like those of quicksilver; whence it becomes extremely moveable and penetrating. Thus it readily enters the pores of wood, leather, skins, chords, and musical strings, and is capable of moving and agitating particles of matter less active than itself; and so proves the more immediate physical agent of fermentation, putrefaction, solution, and the like; and thus it also conveys earthy and saline matter through filtres of paper, stone, &c. and even raises some proportion of them in distillations. Its particles appear to be extremely minute, and so have a large share of surface. Hence water is admirably fitted for solvent, or for readily entering the pores of salts, and coming into full contact with all their particles; and thus it will pass where air cannot, on account of its moisture, or lubricating power, whereby it fastens mucilaginous matters, and will therefore soke through the close pores of a bladder. It penetrates the atmosphere very copiously, by means of the continual distillations of the ocean and rivers, raised up by the heat of the central sun, and draws along with it a warm unctious vapour, which causes a natural generation of whatever the earth, as a matrix, is impregnated with. Water always contains an earthy substance, and is found in the hardest bodies, and in the driest air. It is the proper menstruum of salts, and, by the readiness with which it imbibes the different kinds of air, is easily rendered, by a lately-discovered chemical process, to possess the same qualities and virtues of the most esteemed mineral waters hitherto discovered. Water is also of infinite use in all the works both of nature and art, as without it there could be no generation, nutrition, or accretion, performed in any of the animal, vegetable, mineral, marine, or atmospherical, regions. The blood could not flow in the veins, the sap in the vessels of vegetables, nor the particles of minerals concrete and grow together, without water. It is this that makes the largest part of our blood, our drink, and other aliments. There could be no corruption, fermentation, or dissolution, carried on without it; no brewing, no distilling, no wines, no vinegar, no spirits, made without it. We also meet with water under an infinite variety of forms, and in an infinite variety of bodies, as that of air, vapour, clouds, snow, hail, ice, sap, wines, blood, flesh, bone, horn, stone, and other bodies, through all which it seems to pass unaltered, as an agent or instrument that suffers no alteration by re-action, but remains capable of resuming the form of water again upon any occasion. In its own common state, water appears to be a combination of all the elements together, as containing a quantity of fire, which keeps it fluid; a quantity of air, and a quantity of earth; whence it is not at all surprising, that water alone, as it appears to the senses, should suffice for vegetation in some cases, where little earth is wanted, or for supporting animal and mineral life, where no great degree of nutriment is required; and hence it proves a glue on cement to some bodies, a solvent to others; thus it consolidates brick, plaister of Paris, stone, bone, and the like; but dissolves salts, and subtile earth approaching to salts, and becomes the instrumental cause of their action. Water also conveys nourishment or a more fixed and solid matter to the parts of vegetables, where having deposited it, the finer fluid perspires into the atmosphere, which gives us the physical cause of the dampness and unwholesomeness of woody countries, as they remarkably find in America. For all large vegetables act after the manner of forcing-pumps, continually drawing in large quantities of water at their roots, and discharging it at their leaves; which intimates a method of collecting water in dry countries, and likewise of making salt water fresh. It is also observable, that water in passing through plants, after having deposited its more terrestrial part, does not always go off pure, but impregnated with the finer effluvia, or more subtile particles, of the vegetable; thus making an atmosphere around every plant according to its nature, odoriferous or otherwise, which supplies us with a rule for procuring the odoriferous waters of vegetables by distillation. But the particles, not fine enough to go off thus along with the water, are left behind upon the surface of the leaves and flowers of plants, being now thickened or drained from their moister parts, and remaining in the form of honey, manna, gums, or balsams, according to the nature of the vegetable. And hence we deduce the physical cause why plants prove more odoriferous and sweet when the air is both warm and moist, as is the case immediately after a summer shower. Water is likewise of the utmost use in divers of the mechanical arts and occasions of life; as in the motion of mills, engines, fountains, and all other machines which act by the laws of Hydrostatics.—-For the further properties and effects of Water, see Desag. Exp. Phil. vol. ii. Cotes's Hyd. and Pneum. Lectures. Phil. Trans. No. 203, 220,337. Ferguson's Lectures, 4m. p. 68, &c. Chamb. Cyclop. Art. Water, Fluids, Hydrostatics, &c.

The fourth element, which is passive and fixed, is Earth, and consists of a simple, dry, and cold, substance; and is an ingredient in the composition of all natural bodies. It must be observed, that pure native earth is a very different matter from the earth whereon we tread, and this pure earth is supposed to be the basis or substratem of all bodies, and that wherein the other principles reside. It is all that is solid in an animal or vegetable body, all the real vascular parts, the rest being juices. This earth may be found in and separated from all animal and vegetable substances, and is the same in all, and is the basis of all. It remains after the separation of the other principles, by chemistry, from all animal and vegetable subtances, and neither coheres together, nor differs any change in the fire. The assayers acknowledge no difference between the earth of animals and vegetables, but make their tests for the nicest uses equally of both. If water be poured upon this earth, it requires some degree of tenacity, so as to become capable of being formed into vessels; but, if oil be added, it coheres into a much stronger and more compact mass; hence it appears that oil and earth are the principles which give confidence and tenacity to plants. This oil, as well as this earth, seems the same in all, and possesses nothing of the poisonous or medicinal virtues of the plant, or whatever it is extracted from; they being all separable by decoction, distillation, and other processes of that kind, and never remain either in the earth, or in this connecting oil. Long drying will divest plants of all their virtues; so that nothing but these principles shall remain in them, and these, giving solidity and figure, preserve the plant in its former appearance; but, these only remaining, it possesses none of its virtues. This pure earth may be procured by drawing off the spirit, sulphur, phlegm, and salts, of wine; and what remains will be a tasteless, scentless, dusty, matter, not capable of being raised by distillation, or dissolved by solution, but will preserve the same state and form even in the fire; and this is called pure earth, or *caput mortum*. It may also be obtained pure and unmixed from the common class of vegetables and other bodies, by letting the remaining mass, after distillation, be thoroughly calcined, then boiled in several waters to get out all its salt, and after this dried in a clear fire, or in the sun; and this dried mass will be pure earth. Thus, from the different qualities and operations of the four elements upon one another, we may observe, that the fire preserves the earth from being overwhelmed or destroyed by water; the air preserves the fire, that it is not extinguished; and the water preserves the earth, that it is not burnt; but, if either of these active elements were to become predominant in any great degree, the world would be destroyed; as was the case at the time of the deluge, by the predominancy of water.——For more on this subject, see Boerhaave's Chemist. part ii. p. 21. Shaw's Lectures, p. 151, Phil. Trans. No. 3. Hill's Hill, of Foslils. Linn. Syst. Nat. tom. iii. 1770. Da Costa's Fossils, p. 119, &c. Swed. Mem. 1760.

Of these four elements the whole terrestrial world is composed, with all its productions and appendages; and over these Man hath the dominion, as God's vicegerent upon earth, being compounded of the most perfect and noble part of earthly matter, and formed after God's own image and likeness. Hence man is called the Microcosm, from μιχρος, *little*, and χοσμος, *world*, literally signifying, *the little world*, which is applied to Man by way of eminence, as being an epitome of all that is excellent and wonderful in Nature. If we attentively consider the structure and faculties of man, we shall clearly perceive his existence upon earth, in a character subordinate to that of angels, is only intended by the Deity for a state of probation; and, as this corporeal life shall terminate, either in acts of piety or profaneness, so shall follow the retributions of an impartial and just Judge, in a future state of everlasting duration. Man is composed of three distinct essences, Spirit, Soul, and Body: as St. Paul evinces when he says. *Let your Spirits, Souls, and Bodies, be kept blameless at the coming of the Lord Jesus Christ*. And these three essences are compounded of the three lesser worlds; the Soul of Man is formed of the ethereal world; the Spirit, of the celestial world; and the Body, of the elementary world. Hence are deducible the influences of the sun, moon, and stars, upon Man's body, because he hath a microcosmical sun, moon, and stars, within himself, that bear a sympathy with the celestial bodies, and in the centre of which shines the divine Spirit. For the sensual, celestial, part of man, is that whereby we move, see, feel, taste, and smell, and have a commerce with all material objects; and through these the influences of the divine Nature are conveyed to the more refined and sensible organs. This celestial spirit actuates and influences the elementary essence, and stirs it up to the propagation of its like, and to every other purpose for which Nature designed it. And this spirit is even discoverable in herbs and flowers, which open when the sun rises, and close when he sets; which motion is produced by the spirit being sensible of the approach and departure of the sun's influence. Next to these, in Man, shines that pure, etherial, angelic part, called the rational soul; which is a divine light or stream flowing immediately from the Great Creator, uniting Man with God, and raising him above all other parts of animated nature. This Soul, when once it enters the body, runs parallel with eternity; and joins in with the celestial spirit, through the sphere of the planets; and is conducted by a divine genius, to an hypostatical union with the elementary body; so that there exist two active principles in the body of man to one passive; and, as the Superior Rules in the celestial world are situated at the time of man's nativity, so will his constitution and disposition be framed. And here we derive the cause of all those astonishing variations of temper, disposition, and constitution, which are not only peculiar to different subjects, but even to one and the same person; for every one will bear testimony of this fact, that we find ourselves sometimes chearful, and at other times melancholy; to-day in perfect health, and to-morrow in pain and anguish; this hour composed, affable, and complaisant, and the next austere, petulant, and peremptory; and these contrarieties are evidently produced by the continual resistance and opposition of the four elements in man's body, which alternately dispose him to the various affections discoverable in human nature. The cause of this is induced from the natural enmity of the elementary matter, viz. heat and cold, and driness and moisture; each of which occasionally predominates in man's body, according to the motion and influence of those heavenly bodies, that rule, govern, and modify, the operation of the four elements, in and upon every terrestrial substance. Thus it is evident, that the understanding and intellectual faculties of Man are formed of the ethereal world; the sensitive powers of life and action are derived from the celestial world; and the gross and corruptible part, the flesh and blood, consists of the elementary world; which are all subordinate the one to the other. Under this idea of the workmanship and construction of Man, Job exclaimed, that *he was fearfully and wonderfully made*; in possessing the three-fold essences of spirit, soul, and body.

Sceptical and atheistical writers, indeed, have attempted to overturn this system of nature in the construction of man, by denying the immortality of the soul, and a future distribution of rewards and punishments; contending that the soul is an indivisible part of the body, and has its dissolution in the common course of mortality. But these tenets are so extremely absurd, so vague, and so destitute of evidence, that the rational mind is at a loss to conceive how such an inconsistent doctrine could have ever been broached; for, the same philosophical reasoning, that enables us to define the nature and exigence of the body, will likewise prove the nature and existence of the soul. It is only from the primary or essential qualities of body, its extension, and solidity, that we form any idea of it; and why may we not form the complex idea of a soul or spirit, from the operations of thinking, understanding, willing, and the like, which are experiments in ourselves? This idea of an immaterial substance is as clear as that we have of a material one; for, though the notion of immaterial substances may be attended with difficulties, we have no more reason to deny or doubt of its truth, than we have to deny or doubt of the existence of the body. That the soul is an immaterial substance, appears from hence—that the primary operations of willing and thinking are not only unconnected with the known properties of body, but seem plainly inconsistent with some of its most essential qualities. For the mind not only discovers no relation between thinking and the motion and arrangement of parts; but it likewise perceives, that conciousness, a simple act, can never proceed from a compounded substance capable of being divided into many parts. To illustrate this, let us only suppose a system of matter endowed with thought; then, either all the parts of which this system consists must think, which would make it not one, but a multitude of distinct conscious beings, or its power of thinking must arise from the connection of the parts one with another, their motion, and disposition, which, all taken together, contribute to the production of thought. But it is evident, that the motion of parts, and the manner of combining them, can produce nothing but an artful structure, and various modes of motion. Hence all machines, however artfully their parts are put together, and however complicated their structure, though we conceive innumerable different motions, variously combined, and running one into another with an endless variety, yet never produce any thing but figure and motion. If a clock, or watch, tells the hour and minute of the day, it is only by the motion of the different hands, pointing successively at the different figures marked upon the dial-plate for that purpose. We never imagine this to be the effect of thought or intelligence, nor conceive it possible, by any refinement of structure, so to improve the composition, as that it shall become capable of knowledge and consciousness; and the reason is plainly this, that thought being something altogether different from motion and figure, without the least connection between them, it can never be supposed to result from them. This then being evident, that intelligence cannot arise from an union or combination of unintelligent parts; if we suppose it to belong to any system of matter, we must necessarily attribute it to all the parts of which that system is composed; whereby, instead of one, we shall, as was before observed, have a multitude of distinct conscious beings. And because matter, how far soever we pursue the minuteness of its parts, is still capable of repeated divisions, even to infinity, it is plain that this absurdity will follow us through all the suppositions that make thought inherent in a material substance. Wherefore, as consciousness is incompatible with the cohesion of solid separable parts, we are necessarily led to place it in some other substance of distinct Nature and Properties—and this substance we call Spirit, which is altogether distinct from body, nay, and commonly placed in opposition to it; for which reason, the beings of this class are called immaterial; a word that implies nothing of their true nature, but merely denotes its contrariety to that of matter, or material substances.

As to the immortality of the human soul, the argument to prove it may be reduced to the following heads; first, The nature of the soul itself, its desires, sense of moral good and evil, and gradual increase of knowledge and perfection; and secondly, The moral attributes of God. Under the former of these considerations, it is apparent that the soul, being an immaterial intelligent substance, as has been already proved, does not depend upon the body for its existence; and therefore may, and absolutely must, exist after the body, unless annihilated by the same power which gave it a being at first, which is not to be supposed, since there are no instances of annihilation in nature. This argument, especially if the infinite capacity of the soul, its strong desire after immortality, its rational activity and advancement towards perfection, be likewise considered, will appear perfectly conclusive to men of a philosophical turn; because nature, or rather the God of nature, does nothing in vain. But arguments drawn from the moral attributes of the Deity are not only better adapted to convince men unacquainted with abstract reasoning, but equally certain and conclusive with the former; for, as the justice of God can never suffer the wicked to escape unpunished, nor the good to remain always unrewarded; therefore arguments drawn from the manifest and continual prosperity of the wicked, and the frequent misfortunes and unhappiness of good and virtuous men in this life, must convince every thinking person, that there is a future state wherein all will be set right, and God's attributes of wisdom, goodness, and justice, fully vindicated. Had the religious and conscientious part of mankind no hopes of a future state, they would be of all men the most miserable; but, as this is absolutely inconsistent with the moral characterer of the Deity, the certainty of such a state is clear to a demonstration.

Thus far we have considered the elementary world, which is the lowest In dignity; and man, the chief subject thereof. The celestial world, which is next in eminence, is constituted of a body natural, most simple, spherical, clear, fluid, and moving constantly in a circle, and this by virtue of an innate power always within itself; comprehending and containing the sun, moon, planets, and stars, fixed in distinct orbs by the great Architect of Nature, and bearing sympathy with all terrestrial substances, as being formed out of the same chaotic mass at the beginning of the world. This celestial heaven is what Moses calls *dakign*, the firmament, which was the work of the second day's creation, and literally signifies an *expanse* or *extension*; a term very well adapted by the prophet to the impression which the heavens make on our senses; whence in other parts of the Scriptures, the heaven is compared to a curtain, or a tent stretched out to dwell in. Through the medium of this celestial world, and the heavenly bodies therein contained, the supreme Being rules, governs, and actuates, the elementary world; and this is apparent, because that thing which we term obedience is only to be found in elementary bodies. And since motion is the cause of all mutation and change, and as all motion originates with the heavenly bodies, by the revolutions of which even Time itself is measured out and divided, so we find these celestial influences produce all the variations of heat and cold, driness and moisture, generation and corruption, increase and decrease, life and death, and all the vicissitudes of nature, without even varying themselves, or being subject to the least change or alteration; whilst the elementary bodies are perpetually changing, and never continue in one stay. Hence it is apparent that the celestial bodies are active, and the elementary passive; so that the celestial bodies give the form and stamp to all the productions of nature, and the elementary bodies subminister matter to receive this form. And as the positions and affections of the heavenly aspects are when this form or stamp is given, and as the quality of the elementary matter shall be when subministered, so will the nature and quality of the subject be, that receives this celestial form or stamp. And, were it not for this active and passive principle, then would all elementary things be alike, without a possibility of existing. It is, therefore, a perfect knowledge of this mediate or celestial world, its various affections and dispositions, the nature, tendency, and effect, of the luminaries, their motions, aspects, and positions, which enable us to judge of future contingencies, and to discover the secret and abstruse operations of nature. But, to attain this knowledge in any competent degree, we must trace these heavenly intelligencers throughout the whole celestial regions, and acquaint ourselves with their general and essential qualities. I shall for this purpose, after treating of the ethereal world, make this speculation a leading clue to the art of calculating nativities.

The ethereal world, which is the superior, and the highest in dignity, is that which the inspired writers, and the ancient philosophers, called the Empyrean Heaven, and is conceived to be the abode of God, and blessed spirits, of angels, and the souls of the righteous departed; wherein the Deity is pleased to afford a nearer and more immediate view of himself, a more sensible manifestation of his glory, and a more adequate perception of his attributes, than in the other parts of the universe, where he is likewise present. But the most exalted conceptions we can possibly form of this blissful abode, are extremely inadequate and imperfect; nor is it in the power of the most enlarged understanding to frame suitable ideas of the Godhead, or of the angelic host that perpetually surround his throne. As much, however, as the human comprehension is able to contain, the Almighty has been graciously pleased to reveal to us in the Scriptures, by the inspired writers, particularly Isaiah, Ezekiel, and St. John the Divine, who have given us very magnificent descriptions of the heavenly mansions, their structure, apparatus, and angelic attendance. From this divine Revelation the Hebrew writers, and other learned men, have described the Harmony of the Universe, and the necessary subordination and dependence of one thing upon another, from the interior heaven to the remotest corner of the earth. We shall therefore presume to follow these authors in speaking of God and his angels; and whoever sufficiently contemplates the subject will be secure against the impious doctrines of Atheists, of Free-thinkers, of immoral and irreligious men.

God is an immaterial, intelligent, and free Being; of perfect goodness, wisdom, and power; who made the universe, and continues to support it, as well as to govern and direct it by his providence. By his immateriality, intelligence, and freedom, God is distinguished, from fate, nature, destiny, necessity, chance, and from all other imaginary beings. In scripture, God is defined by, I am that I am; Alpha and Omega; the beginning and end of all things. Among philosophers, he is defined a Being of infinite perfection; or in whom there is no defect of any thing which we conceive might raise, improve, or exalt, his nature. Among men, he is chiefly considered as the first cause, the first Being, who has existed from the beginning, has created the world, or who subsists necessarily, or of himself; and this knowledge of God, his nature, attributes, word, and works, with the relations between him and his creatures, make the extensive subject of Theology, the sister science of Astrology.

Sir Isaac Newton considers and defines God, not is usually done, from his perfection, his nature, exigence, or the like; but from his dominion. The word God, according to him, is a relative term, and has a regard to servants; it is true it denotes a Being eternal, infinite, and absolutely perfect; but a Being, however eternal, infinite, and absolutely perfect, without dominion, would not be God. The same author observes, that the word God frequently signifies Lord, but every lord is not God; it is the dominion of a spiritual being, or lord, that constitutes God; true dominion, true God; supreme, the supreme; feigned, the false god. From such true dominion it follows, that the true God is living, intelligent, and powerful; and from his other perfections, that he is supreme, or supremely perfect: he is eternal, and infinite; omnipotent, and omniscient; that is, he endures from eternity to eternity, and is present from infinity to infinity. He governs all things that exist, and knows all things that are to be known; he is not eternity, nor infinity, but eternal, and infinite; he is not duration or space, but he endures, and is present; he endures always, and is present every where; and, by existing always, and every where, he constitutes the very thing, duration and space, eternity and infinity. He is omnipresent, not only virtually, but also substantially; for power without substance cannot subsist. All things are contained, and move in him, but without any mutual passion; he suffers nothing from the motions of bodies; nor do they undergo any resistance from his omnipresence. It is confessed that God exists necessarily; and by the same necessity he exists always, and every where. Hence, also, he must be perfectly similar; all eye, all ear, all brain, all arm, all the power of perceiving, understanding, and acting; but after a manner not at all corporeal, after a manner not like that of men, after a manner wholly to us unknown. He is destitute of all body, and all bodily shape; and therefore cannot be seen, heard, or touched; nor ought to be worshipped under the representation of any thing corporeal. We have ideas of the attributes of God, but do not know the substance even of any thing; we see only the figures and colours of bodies, hear only sounds, touch only the outward surfaces, smell only odours, and taste tastes; but do not, cannot, by any sense, or any reflex act, know their inward substances; and much less can we have any notion of the substance of God. We know him by his properties and attributes; by the most wise and excellent structure of things, and by final causes; but we adore and worship him only on account of his dominion; for God, setting aside dominion, providence, and final causes, is nothing else but fate and * nature.

The admirable metaphysician and divine, Dr. Clarke, has demonstrated the being of a God, with that clearness and force of reasoning for which he is so eminently distinguished, by a series of propositions, mutually connected and dependent, and forming a complete and unanswerable argument in proof of the attributes of the Deity. Something, he says, has existed from all eternity; for, since something now is, something always was: otherwise the things that now are must have been produced out of nothing, absolutely and without cause, which is a plain contradiction in terms. There must have existed from all eternity some one unchangeable and independent Being; or else, there has been an infinite succession of changeable and dependent beings, produced one from another in an endless progression, without any original cause at all. For without, this series of beings can have no cause of its existence, because it includes all things that are or ever were in the universe; nor is any one being in this infinite succession self-existent or necessary, and therefore it can have no reason of its existence within itself; and it was equally possible, that from eternity there should never have existed any thing at all, as that a succession of such beings should have existed from eternity. Consequently their existence is determined by nothing; neither by any necessity in their own nature, because none of them are self-existent; nor by any other being, because no other is supposed to exist.—That unchangeable and independent

---

* See Newton's Philos. Nat. Princip, Math. in calce.

Being, which has existed from eternity, without any external cause of its existence, must be self-existent; it must exist by an absolute necessity originally in the nature of the thing itself, and antecedent in the natural order of our ideas to our supposition of its being. For whatever exists, must either come into being without a cause; or it must have been produced by some external cause; or it must be self-existent: but the two former suppositions are contrary to the two first propositions. From this last proposition it follows, that the only true idea of a self-existent or necessarily existing being, is the idea of a being, the supposition of whose non-existence is an express contradiction; and this idea is that of a most simple being, absolutely eternal and infinite, original and independent. It follows also, that nothing is so certain as the existence of a supreme independent cause; and likewise, that the material world cannot possibly be-the first and original being, uncreated, independent, and of itself eternal; because it does not exist by an absolute necessity in its own nature, so as that it must be an express contradiction to suppose it not to exist. With respect both to its form and matter, the material world may be conceived not to be, or to be in any respect different from what it is without a contradiction. The substance or essence of the self-existent being is absolutely incomprehensible by us; nevertheless, many of the essential attributes of his nature are strictly demonstrable, as well as his existence. The self-existent being, having no cause of its existence but the absolute-necessity of its own nature, must of necessity have existed from everlasting, without beginning; and must of necessity exist to everlasting, without end.—-The self-existent being must of necessity be infinite and omnipresent. Such a being must be every where, as well as always unalterably the same. It follows from hence, that the self-existent being must be a most simple, unchangeable, incorruptible, being, without parts, figure, motion, divisibility, and other properties of matter, which are utterly inconsistent with complete infinity. The self-existent being must of necessity be but one; because in absolute necessity there can be no difference or diversity of existence; and, therefore, it is absolutely impossible, that there should be two independent self-existent principles, such as God and matter.——-The self-existent and original cause of all things must be an intelligent being. This proposition cannot be demonstrated strictly and properly *a priori*; but, *a posteriori*, the world affords undeniable arguments to prove that all things are the effects of an intelligent and knowing cause. The cause must be always more excellent than the effect; and, therefore, from the various kinds of powers and degrees of excellence and perfection, which visible objects possess;

from the intelligence of created beings, which is a real distinct quality or perfection, and not a mere effect or composition of unintelligent figure and motion; from the variety, order, beauty, wonderful contrivance, and fitness, of all things to their proper and respective ends; and from the original of motion, the self-existent creating being is demonstrated to be intelligent. The self-existent and original cause of all things is not a necessary agent, but a being endued with liberty and choice. Liberty is a necessary consequent of intelligence.; without liberty, no being can be said to be an agent, or cause of anything; since to act necessarily, is really and properly not to act at all, but to be acted upon. Besides, if the supreme cause be not endued with liberty, it will follow, that nothing which is not could possibly have been; that nothing which is, could possibly not have been; and that no mode or circumstance of the existence of any thing could possibly have been in any respect otherwise than what it now actually is. Farther, if there be any final cause in the universe, the supreme cause is a free agent; and, on the contrary supposition, it is impossible that any effect should be finite; and in every effect there must have been a progression of causes *in infinitum*, without any original cause at all.—The self-existent being, the supreme cause of all things, must of necessity have infinite power; since all things were made by him, and are entirely dependent upon him; and all the powers of all things are derived from him, and perfectly subject to him; nothing can resist the execution of his will.— The supreme cause and author of all things must of necessity be infinitely wise. This follows from the propositions already established; and the proof *a posteriori*, of the infinite wisdom of God, from the consideration of the exquisite perfection and consummate excellency of his works, is no less strong and undeniable.—The supreme cause and author of all things must of necessity be a being of infinite goodness, justice, and truth, and all other moral perfections; such as become the supreme governor and judge of the world. The will of a being, infinitely knowing and wise, independent and all-powerful, can never be influenced by any wrong affection, and can never be misled or opposed from without; and, therefore, he must do always what we know fittest to be done; that is, he must act always according to the strictest rules of infinite goodness, justice, and truth, and all other moral perfections; and more particularly, being infinitely and necessarily happy and all-sufficient, he must be unalterably disposed to do and to communicate good or *happiness.

* See Clarke's Demonstration of the Being and Attributes of God.

To this more abstruse argument *a priori*, for the existence of God, we may add another, more generally obvious, and carrying irresistible conviction, which is deduced from the frame of the world, and from the traces of evident contrivance and fitness of things for one another that occur through all the parts of it. These conspire to prove, that the material world, which in its nature is originated and dependent, could not have been the effect of chance or necessity, but of intelligence and design. The beautiful, harmonious, and beneficial, arrangement of the various bodies that compose the material system; their mutual dependence and subserviency; the regularity of their motions, and the aptitude of these motions for producing the most beneficial effects; and many other phenomena resulting from their relation, magnitude, situation, and use, afford unquestionable evidences of the creating power and wise disposal of an intelligent and almighty agent. The power of gravity, by which the celestial bodies persevere in their revolutions, deserves our particular consideration. This power penetrates to the centres of the sun and planets, without any diminution of its virtue, and is extended to immense distances, regularly decreasing, and producing the most sensible and important effects. Its action is proportional to the quantity of solid matter in bodies, and not to their surfaces, as is usual in mechanical causes; and, therefore, seems to surpass mere mechanism. But however various the phenomena that depend on this power, and may be explained by it, no mechanical principles can account for its effects; much less could it have produced, at the beginning, the regular situation of the orbs, and the present disposition of things. Gravity could not have determined the planets to move from west to east, in orbits nearly circular, almost in the same plane; nor could their power have projected the comets, with all the variety of their directions. If we suppose the matter of the system to be accumulated the centre by its gravity, no mechanical principles, with the assistance of this power, could separate the huge and unwieldy mass into such parts as the sun and planets; and, after carrying them to their different distances, project them in their several directions, preserving still the equality of action and reaction, or the state of the centre of gravity of the system. Such an exquisite structure of things could only arise from the contrivance and powerful influences of an intelligent, free, and most potent, agent. The same powers, therefore, which at present govern the material world, and conduct its various motions, are very different from those, which were necessary to have produced it from nothing, or to have disposed it in the admirable form in which it now proceeds.

But we should exceed the limits of our plan, if, confining our observation to the earth, our own habitation, we were to enumerate only the principal traces of design and wisdom, as well as goodness, which are discernible in its figure and constituent parts, in its diurnal and annual motion, in the position of its axis with regard to its orbit, in the benefit which it derives from the light and heat of the sun, and the alternate vicissitudes of the seasons; in the atmosphere which surrounds it, and in the different species and varieties of vegetables and animals with which it is replenished. No one can survey the vegetable productions of the earth, so various, beautiful, and useful, nor the various gradations of animal life, in such a variety of species, all preserved distinct, and propagated by a settled law, each fitted to its own element, provided with proper food, and with instincts and organs suited to its rank and situation, and especially with the powers of sensation and self-motion, and all more immediately or remotely subservient to the government and use of man, without admiring the skill and design of the original Former. But these are more signally manifested in the structure of the human frame, and in the noble powers and capacities of the human mind; more especially in the moral principles and faculties, which are a distinguishing part of our constitution, and lead to the perception and acknowledgement of the existence and government of God. In those instances that have now been recited, and a variety of similar instances suggested by them, or naturally occurring to the notice of the curious and reflecting mind, contrivance is manifest, and immediately, without any nice or subtle reasoning, suggests a contriver. It strikes us like a sensation; and artful reasonings against it may puzzle us, without shaking our belief. No person, for example, that knows the principles of optics, and the structure of the eye, can believe that it was formed without skill in that science; or that the ear was formed without the knowledge of sounds; or that the male and female, created and preserved in due proportion, were not formed for each other, and for continuing the species. All our accounts of nature are full of instances of this kind. The admirable and beautiful structure of things for final causes exalts our idea of the contriver; and the unity of design shews him to be one. The great motions in the system, performed with the same facility as the least, suggest his almighty power, which gave motion to the earth and the celestial bodies with equal ease as to the minutest particles; the subtility of the motions and actions in the internal parts of bodies, shews that his influence penetrates the inmost recesses of things, and that he is equally active and present every where. The simplicity of the laws that prevail in the world, the excellent disposition of things, in order to obtain the best ends, and the beauty which adorns the works of nature, far superior to any thing in art, suggest his consummate wisdom. The usefulness of the whole scheme, so well contrived for the intelligent beings who enjoy it, with the internal disposition and moral structure of those beings, shews his unbounded goodness. These are arguments which are sufficiently open to the views and capacities of the unlearned, while at the same time they acquire new strength and lustre from the discoveries of the learned. The Deity's acting and interposing in the universe, shew that he governs it, as well as that he formed it; and the depth of his counsels, even in conducting the material universe, of which a great part surpasses our knowledge, tends to preserve an inward veneration and awe of this great Being, and disposes us to receive what may be otherwise revealed to us concerning him. His essence, as well as that of all other substances, is beyond the reach of all our discoveries; but his attributes clearly appear in his admirable works. We know that the highest conceptions we are able to form of them are still beneath his real perfections; but his dominion over us, and our duty towards him, are abundantly* manifest.

Another substantial argument to prove the existence of God, as the creator and governor of the universe, may be deduced from the universal consent of mankind, and the uniform tradition of this belief through every nation and every age; it is impossible to conceive, that a fallacy, so perpetual and universal, should be imposed on the united reason of mankind. No credible and satisfactory account can be given of this universal consent, without ascribing it to the original constitution of the human mind, in consequence of which it cannot fail to discern the existence of a Deity, and to the undeniable traces of his being, which his works afford. Fear, state-policy, and the prejudices of education, to which the concurrence of mankind in this principle has been sometimes resolved, are founded on this universal principle, suppose its being an influence, and are actuated by it. It is much more reasonable to imagine, that the belief of a God was antecedent to their operation, than that it should have been produced by them; and that it was dictated by reason and conscience, independent of the passion and policy of men. The uniform and universal tradition of this belief, and of the creation of the world by

---

* See Maclaurin's Account of Sir Isaac Newton's Phil. Dis. b. iv. chap. 9. Baxter in his Matho, Derham, Ray, Niewentyt, De la Pluche in his Nature Displayed, Chamn. Cyclop. &c.

the divine power, affords concurring evidence both of the principle and of the fact. The existence of God is also farther evinced by those arguments which have been usually alledged to prove, that the world had a beginning, and, therefore, that it must have been created by the energy of divine power. In proof of this, the history of Moses, considered merely as the most ancient historian, deserves particular regard. His testimony is confirmed by the most ancient writers, among the heathens, both poets and historians. It may be also fairly alledged, that we have no history or tradition more ancient than that which agrees with the received opinion of the world's beginning, and of the manner in which it was produced; and that the most ancient histories were written long after that time. And this consideration is urged by Lucretius, the famous Epicurean, as a strong presumption that the world had a beginning:

-Si nulla fuit genitalis origo

Terrarum & coeli, semperque aeterna fuere:

Cur supra bellum Thebanum, & funera Trojae,

Non alias alii quoque res cecinere poetae?*

Besides, the origin and progress of learning, and the most useful arts, confirm the notion of the world's beginning, and of the common aera of its creation; to which also may be added, that the world itself, being material and corruptible, must have had a beginning; and many phenomena occur to the observation of the astronomer and mathematician, which furnish a strong presumption, that it could have had no long duration, and that it now gradually tends to dissolution. From these considerations we may infer the absolute being and providence of God; which also demonstrate the existence of his angels and ministring spirits, who are the messengers of his will, and the proper inhabitants of the ethereal world, and consequently the next subjects of our enquiry.

---

* [If nothing has a reproductive origin
Of earth and heaven, always being eternal
But why of the Theban war before, and ruin of Troy
Have other poets not likewise sung of other things?

Lucretius De Rerum Natura 5: 324-327]

An Angel is a spiritual intelligent substance, and the first in rank and dignity of all created beings; though the word *Angel*, Αυγελος, is not properly a denomination of nature, but of office; denoting a *messenger*, or *executioner* of the will of some superior power or authority. In this sense they are frequently mentioned in Scripture, as ministring spirits sent by the Almighty to declare his will, and to correct, teach, reprove, and comfort. God also promulgated the law to Moses, and appeared to the old patriarchs by the mediation of angels, who represented him, and spoke in his name. The existence of angels is admitted in all religions; the Greeks and Latins acknowledged them under the names of genii and demons; and in the Alcoran we find frequent mention of them; the professors of the Mahometan religion assigned them various orders and degrees, as well as different employments, both in heaven and on earth. The Sadducees also admit their existence: witness Abusaid, the author of an Arabic version of the Pentateuch; and Aaron, a Caraite Jew, in his comment on the Pentateuch; both extant in manuscript in the king of France's library. The heathen philosophers and poets were also agreed as to the existence of intelligent beings, superior to man; as is shewn by St. Cyprian, in his treatise on the vanity of idols, from the testimonies of Plato, Socrates, and Trismegistus. Authors are not so unanimous about their nature as of their existence; Clemens Alexandrinus believed they had bodies, which was also the opinion of Origen, Caesarius, Tertullian, and several others; but Athanasius, Basil, Gregory, Nicene, Cyril, and Chrysostom, hold them to be mere spirits. Authors are also divided as to the time of the creation of angels; some will have it to have been before the creation of our world, or ever from eternity; while others maintain that they were created at the same time with our world. The most probable conjecture is, that they were created at different periods, whenever it pleased the Almighty to call them into existence. But, though we cannot so clearly demonstrate the precise nature and duration of angels, we may nevertheless conclude, that, though they are of an order highly superior to that of men, yet are they not complete and perfect; for, had they been created thus originally, they could not have fallen, as Adam did, nor have sinned, which the scriptures inform us some of them did, by rebelling against the Almighty, and in contending with him for supreme authority. For this reason, as they are themselves imperfect beings, they can in no one respect be considered proper objects of human adoration, which we are bound to pay alone to that ONE SUPREME, who is omnipotent, immortal, infinite, the source and centre of every thing that is great, and good, and perfect.

Theologists have divided angels into different ranks or subordinations, which they term Hierarchies, from ιερος, *holy*, and αρχε, *rule*, signifying, *holy command*, or *to rule in holy things*. Dionysius and other ancient writers have established nine choirs or orders of these celestial spirits, namely, seraphim, cherubim, thrones, dominions, principalities, powers, virtues, angels, and archangels; and these they form into three Hierarchies, appointing them their respective offices in the performance of adoration and praise, and in executing the word and will of God. The Rabbins and Jewish writers, who had obviously a more immediate knowledge of the angelic host, by the inspiration of their prophets, and the revelation of God's true religion, have defined one rank of angels, or intelligent beings, superior to all the foregoing, which answer to or are contained in the ten distinguishing names of God, and are the pure essences of his spirit, or stream though which his will and pleasure is communicated to the angels and blessed spirits, and through which his providence extends to the care and protection of all his works. The first of these divine effences is denominated יהוה, *Jehovah*, and is peculiarly attributed to God the Father, being the pure and simple essence of the Divinity, flowing through Hajoth Hakados to the angel Metratton, and to the ministering spirit Reschith Hagalalim, who guides the *primum mobile*, and bestows the gift of being upon all things. To this spirit is allotted the office of bringing the souls of the faithful departed into heaven; and by him God spake to Moses. The second is יה *Jah*, and is attributed the person of the Messiah, or Λογος, whose power and influence descends though the angel Masleh into the sphere of the Zodiac. This is the spirit or word which actuated the chaos, and divided the unwrought matter into three portions: of the first or most essential part was the spiritual world composed; of the second was made the visible heavens and the luminous bodies; and of the third or inferior part was formed the terrestrial world, out of which was drawn the elemental quintessence or first matter, of all things, which produced the four elements, and all creatures that inhabit them, by the agency of a particular spirit called Raziel, who was the ruler of Adam. The third is אהיה, *Ehjeh*, and is attributed to the Holy Spirit, whose divine light is received by the angel Sabbathi, and communicated from him through the sphere of Saturn. This is the *principum generationis*, the beginning of the ways of God, or the manifestation of the Father and the Son's light in the supernatural generation. And from hence flow down all living souls, entering the inanimate body, and giving form to unsettled matter. The fourth is אל, *El*, through the light of whom flow grace, goodness, mercy, piety, and munificence, to the angel Zadkiel; and, thence passing through the sphere of Jupiter, fashioneth the images of all bodies, bestowing clemency, benevolence, and justice, on all. The fifth is אלהי, *Elohi*, the upholder of the sword, and left-hand of God, whose influence penetrates the angel Geburah, and thence descends though the sphere of Mars, giving fortitude in war and affliction. The sixth is צבאות, *Tsebaoth*, who bestoweth his mighty power through the angel Raphael into the sphere of the Sun, giving motion, heat, and brightness, to it, and thence producing metals. The seventh is עליון, *Elion*, who rules the angel Michael, and descends though the sphere of Mercury, giving benignity, motion, and intelligence, with elegance and consonance of speech. The eighth is ארובי, *Adonai*, whose influence is received by the angel Haniel, and communicated through the sphere of Venus, giving zeal, fervency, and righteousness of heart, and producing vegetables. The ninth is שרי, *Shaddai*, whose influence is conveyed by cherubim to the angel Gabriel, and falls into the sphere of the Moon, causing increase and decrease of all things, governing the genii and protectors of men. The tenth is אלהים, *Elohim*, who extends his beneficence to the angel Jesodoth, into the sphere of the earth, and dispenseth knowledge, understanding, and wisdom. The three first of these ten names, viz. יהוה, Jehovah, יה, Jah, and אהיה, Ehjeh, express the essence of God, and are proper names; but the other seven are only expressive of his attributes. The principal and only true name of the Godhead, according both to the Hebrews and and Greeks, is בנאדנצאאותירוה, Τετραγραμματον, *the name of four letters*, with which the Godhead, in most languages, is observed to be expressed; thus in Hebrew the Supreme Being is called יהוה Jehovah; in the Greek, θεος; in Latin, *Deus*; it Spanish, *Dios*; in Italian, *Idio*; in French, *Dieu*; in the ancient Gaulish, *Diex*; in ancient German, *Diet*; in the Sclavonic, *Buch*; in Arabic, *Alla*; in the Polish, *Bung*; in the Pannonian, *Istu*; in the Egyptian, *Tenu*; in the Persian, *Sire*; and in the language of the ancient Magi, *Orsi*. Thus God is conceived to work by the ideas of his own mind, and these ideas dispense their seals, and communicate them to whatever is formed or created.

In the exterior circle of the celestial heaven, in which are placed the fixed stars, the *Anima Mundi* hath her particular forms, or seminal conceptions, answering to the ideas of the Divine Mind; and this situation, approaching nearest to the empyrean heaven, the seat of God, receives the spiritual powers and influences which immediately proceed from him. Hence they are diffused through the spheres of the planets and heavenly bodies, and communicated to the inmost centre of the earth, by means of the terrestrial elements. Thus have the wise and learned men among the Jews deduced the construction and harmony of the world, and shewn that God performs all his secret and stupendous works by the medium of the celestial bodies. He acts and governs immediately by himself, but mediately by the heavenly bodies, which are the instruments of his Providence, and the secondary causes, by which the earth and all similar systems are regulated; and these, perhaps, regulate one another, by a reciprocal influence and sympathy, communicated to them in the ordination of nature. And hence comes the original or groundwork of all men's nativities, and all manner of natural questions and things, and the story of all that may happen or proceed out of natural causes, to the full end of time. To demonstrate this more satisfactorily, we shall now define the natural properties of the celestial world, with its particular divisions, quantity, motion, and measure, as laid down by the rules of Astronomy; and this will lead us to the doctrine of nativities.

AN

ILLUSTRATION

OF THE

CELESTIAL SCIENCE

OF

ASTROLOGY

PART the FOURTH.

CONTAINING THE

DISTINCTION between ASTROLOGY

AND THE

WICKED PRACTICE of EXORCISM.

WITH A GENERAL DISPLAY OF

WITCHCRAFT, MAGIC, and DIVINATION,

FOUNDED UPON THE

EXISTENCE of SPIRITS Good and Bad, and
their
AFFINITY with the Affairs of this WORLD.

By E B E N E Z E R S I B L Y, Astro. Philo.

RE-PRINTED IN THE YEAR MMXIV.

FROM what has been premised in the foregoing parts of this work, it will now become manifest to every unprejudiced reader, that Astrology and Magic, how much soever they have been confounded with each other, and considered by the vulgar as one and the same doctrine, are nevertheless two very opposite and distinct pursuits. The one not only supposes, but in truth is, an attainment of the contingencies and events of futurity from a natural cause implanted in the motion and influence of the spheres, which it is at once honourable and praiseworthy to study; the other, an acquirement of particular events to come, or mischiefs to be performed, by means of occult spells, diabolical incantations, the agency of spirits, or confederacy with the devil. This constitutes what is termed Magic, Exorcism, Witchcraft, and Divination, very aptly termed "The Black Art," which it shall be the principal object of the following pages to illustrate; as well to give the reader some rational idea of that very ancient but mischievous practice, as to clear the sublime contemplation and study of the stars from the gross imputations it hath on that account sustained.

I have no doubt but the greater part of my readers, and perhaps the bulk of mankind at this day, totally disbelieve the possibility of witchcraft, magic, or divination; because, they deny the very existence of spirits, the agency of the devil, and the appearance of ghosts or spirits of deceased men, upon which belief the practice of the black art entirely depends. But, however incredulous the wisest man may be, as to what has been related on this subject, certain it is, that such spirits really do exist, and that confederacy and compact with them was in former times no uncommon thing. Blackstone seems to have established this fact in a very satisfactory manner, where he speaks of the laws formerly provided in this country against witches, and those who held confederacy with spirits; which to disbelieve, would not only be found to militate against numerous important passages of Scripture, but would call in question the express words of our Saviour himself, and give the lie to authors and attestators of the first reputation and character. Indeed, the force of revelation, and the doctrine of Christ, depends very much upon our opinion of the existence of spirits; for that, being confessed or doubted, either affirms or denies the eternity of the soul.

Those persons, who have taken pains to contemplate the nature and structure of man, will have no difficulty to believe, from the principles of reason and common sense, that a soul, essence, or spirit, absolutely exists within his body, totally independent of all material functions or desires; that flies in his face upon the commission of every unjust or improper act, and that leads the human ideas to a state of being infinitely beyond the bounds of the terrestrial globe, and unconstrained by the limits of time. This applies to the essence, soul, or spirit, of man; whereas the body, being compounded of the elements of this world, is swayed ruled, and eventually overcome, by them, in proportion as the elements operate upon one another, so as to produce diseases, imbecility, and death.

As it is agreed by all authors, and admitted in the creed of all sects and persuasions of people, that, before the fall, the seasons and elements were in one unalterable state of perfection and harmony; so the condition of man was not then under the power of the elements, but he was clothed with purity and immortality as with a garment. The external gross elements had then no sway; and the astral powers, instead of inflaming his desires, contributed unto him the influences of like unto like, forming an union of delectable ideas between soul and body, which led to the unabated praise and adoration of his beneficent Creator. The pure elements were then congeneal to his state of immortality, and the astral powers were turned upon his back, while innocence and incorruptibility smiled on his brow. His food was not limited to palpable matter, but was combined with the pure ethereal spirit of the universe, which perfumed the air, and enriched the seat of paradise.

Such was the primeval happy state of Man. But departing from his innocency, by the secret insinuations infused into his mind by the fallen spirit Satan, he lusted after palpability in the flesh, turned his face to the elememts, deserted his reason and his God, and fell from his ethereal state into all the perils of mortality and death. Having no longer all powers under his subjection, he became subject to sidereal and elementary influx, with his understanding darkened, and his mental faculties abridged; which I have exhibited by the four figures in the annexed plate. The first represents the primeval state of man, with his hand lifted up to his head, denoting the seat of comprehensive sensibility, to which the light of reason and sense flowed from the mirror of the Deity, in whose image he was formed. The second figure shows the elementary and astral influence in the primeval state of man, as having no action whatsoever internally, but falling on his exterior or back parts; whilst his face, turned to the light, received the beatific vision of immortality and life from the gate of heaven. The third figure shows the internal action of the elementary and planetary influx after the fall, upon the vital parts of man, whence diseases and death follow in a direst and regular course. For, as the action of the stars on man are agents, and the elements of which he is composed patients, the same as in the outward world; so we find, as they are situated in the outward world at the time of birth, either as to strength or imbecility, so shall be the inward weakness or vigour of the vital parts of man born under them;

and of such shall be the inbred quality of the disease thus implanted in our fallen nature to bring on corruptibility and death. The fourth figure is intended to show a faint resemblance of an abandoned and more degenerated state of fallen human nature, when the will and passions of man are given up to vice, and contaminated with the gross or bestial quality of deadly sin and wickedness. He is led captive by an evil spirit, the agent of Lucifer, having his will darkened, and every spark of light extinguished, that could flow from the intellectual faculties of the soul, or from the collision of virtue and sense. Such are the men described by St. Paul in his Epistle to the Romans, Chap. i. ver. 28, 29, 30.

In this action of the stars upon man, it leaves the will and the soul totally unconstrained; whilst the body or corruptible part only is influenced, which allures and attracts the will; and, as observation and experience show us, too commonly leads it captive to all the excesses and intemperance of the passions. But, as this is the utmost effect the force of the stars, or the power of the elements, is found to produce in our nature; so the doctrine of Astrology sees no further than to define and explain them through all the tracks of occult speculation and science. Whereas the art of Magic, of Divination, and Exorcism, forms an alliance with the agents of the devil, lusts after compact with damped souls, and holds converse with the departed spirits of men.

To illustrate this extraordinary practice of the ancients, I shall here consider the nature of the World of Spirits, their quality and office, and the affinity which they bear to this world, agreeably to the doctrines laid down by those ancient authors whose works are now rarely to be seen, though fashioned by the most remarkable experiments, and confirmed by the strongest evidence that can be collected at so distant a period.

The noble and learned Swedenborg, whose nativity we have considered in the foregoing part of this work, has with great ingenuity explained the nature and situation of the departed spirits of men, after their recess from this life, " The world of spirits," says this author, " is neither heaven nor hell, but a place or state betwixt both, into which man immediately enters after death; and, after staying there a certain time, longer or shorter, according to what his part life had been in this world, he is either received up into heaven, or call down into hell. It must be noted here, that this intermediate state has nothing in it of the probationary kind; for that is all over with the life of this world; but is a state of *separation*, or reducing every one to his own proper prevailing principle, and as such finally preparatory for an eternal happiness or misery.

"In the world of spirits is always a very great number of them, as being the first sort of all, in order to their examination and preparation; but there is no fixed time for their stay; for some are translated to heaven, and others consigned to hell, soon after their arrival; whilst some continue there for weeks, and others for several years, though none more than thirty, this depending on the correspondence or non-correspondence between the interior and exterior of men. As soon as they arrive in the world of spirits, they are classed according to their several qualities, inclinations, and dispositions: the evil, with such infernal societies as they had communication with in this world, in the ruling passion; and the good, with such heavenly societies as they had communicated with, in love, charity, and faith. But, however they are diversely classed, they all meet and converse together in that world, when they have a desire so to do, who have been friends and acquaintances in this life; more especially husbands and wives, brothers and sisters, &c. But if they are, according to their different ways of life, of different inclinations and habits of mind, they are soon parted; and it may be observed, both concerning those who finally go to heaven, and those that go to hell, that, after their arrival in those two different kingdoms, they no more see or know one another, unless they are of like minds and affections. The reason why they meet and know one another in the world of spirits, and not so in heaven or hell, is because in the world of spirits they pass through the same state they were in in this life, and so from one to another; but afterwards all are fixed in one permanent state respectively, according to the state of that love which prevails in them, in which one knows another from similarity of condition; for similitude joins, but dissimilitude separates.

"As the world of spirits is a middle *state* with man, between heaven and hell, so it is also a middle *place*, having the hells underneath and the heavens above; all the hells are shut next to that world, except that some holes or clefts, like those in rocks or caverns are left open; and those so guarded, that none can pass through them but by permission, which is granted on particular occasions. Heaven like wise, appears as fenced all round, so that there is no passing to any of the heavenly societies but by a narrow way, which is likewise guarded. These outlets and inlets are what in Scripture are called the *doors* and *gates of heaven and hell*.

"The world of spirits appears like a valley, between mountains and rocks, here and there sinking and rising; the doors and gates opening to the heavenly societies are only seen by those who are in their preparation for heaven; nor are they to be found by any others. To every society in heaven there is an entrance from the world of spirits; after passing which, there is a way, which as it rises branches into several others: nor are the doors, and gates of the hells visible to any but those that are going to enter therein, to whom they are then opened; at which time there appear like, as it were, dark and sooty caverns, leading obliquely down to the infernal abyss, where there are also more gates. Through those dark and dismal caverns exhale certain foetid vapours, which are most offensive to the good spirits; but which the evil ones are greedily fond of; for, as were the evils which any one took most delight in when in this worlds, such is the stink corresponding thereto which most pleases him in the other; in which they may be aptly compared to those birds or beasts of prey, as ravens, wolves, and swine, which are attracted by the rank effluvia emitted from carrion and putrid carcasses.

" There, are also in every man two gates, the one of which opens towards hell and to all that is evil and false proceeding therefrom; the other gate opens towards heaven, and to all the good and truth issuing thence. The infernal gate is open to those who are in evil, and they receive from above only some glimmering of heavenly light, just sufficient to serve them to think, reason, and talk of heavenly things; but the gate heaven stands open in those who are good and in truth. There are also two ways leading to the rational mind in man; the superior or internal, by which good and truth are communicated from the Lord; and the inferior or external way, by which evil and falsehood are communicated from hell: and the rational mind is in the midst of these two ways; hence it is, that as much of the heavenly light as any man receiveth into his mind, so far is he truly rational; and so much as he admits not of it, in such proportion he is not rational, however he may think himself so. These things here offered, show the correspondence that subsists between man and heaven and hell; for his rational mind, during the formation of it, corresponds to the world of spirits, things above it being in heaven, and things beneath it in hell; the former are opened, and the latter (as to all influx of good and truth) with respect to those who are in their preparation for hell; consequently the latter can only look down to the things beneath them, or to hell, and the former only to things above them, or to heaven. Now to look up is by correspondence, to look to the Lord, who is the common centre to which all heavenly things point their aspect and tendency; but to look downwards is to turn from the Lord to the opposite centre of attraction, and consequently to all things of a hellish nature. "

"These confederations are applied only to the immediate after-state of the soul and spirit of man, as the consequence of the mortality of this world. Many there are, however, who entirely disbelieve the faculty of the soul, or the existence of the spirit; but whoever rightly considers the matter, cannot but know, that it is not the body, or material part, but the soul, or spiritual part, that thinks within him. Now the soul is his spirit, immortal in all its properties, and receptive of what is spiritual, as having a spiritual life, which consists in thinking and willing; consequently, the whole of the rational life appertains thereto, and not to the body, though manifested therein: for the body is only thoughtless matter, and an adjunct or instrument to the spirit of man, whereby it may manifest its vital powers and functions in this natural world, where all things are material, and as such void of life; it is indeed customary to ascribe action, motion, and power, to the body, in the common forms of speaking; but to suppose that the properties belong to the instrument, and not solely to the principle that actuates it, is erroneous and absurd.

"As all vital power, both of acting and thinking, appertains solely to the spirit, and in no wise to the body, it follows, that the spirit is truly and properly the man, and that without its influence and operation there is neither thought nor life from the crown of the head to the sole of the foot: consequently, that the separation of the body from the spirit, which we call death, takes nothing from that which in reality constitutes the man. For man would not be capable of thinking and willing, unless there were in him a substance to serve as the subject of these operations; and to suppose otherwise would be ascribing existence to non-entity, as may appear from man's not being able to see without that organ which is the subject of vision, or to hear without the organ of hearing; these senses being nothing without such subjects of their operations. Now thought is internal vision, or the sight of the mind, as perception is the internal hearing; and these without internal organized substances, as their proper subjects, cannot exist: so that the spirit of a man has equally a form, and that a human one, as also its sensory and senses, when divested of its material body, as it had before; for all the perceptive life of the eye and the ear, and of every other sense that appertains to man, is not from his material body, but from his spirit and the vital powers thereof, in all and singular the organs and parts of his body: hence it is that spirits see, hear, and feel as well as men, in the spiritual world*, though not in this natural world after their separation from this mortal body. That the spirit had natural sensations in this world, was owing to its union with a natal or material body; but then also it had its spiritual senses in various modes of thinking and willing."

The foregoing doctrine is here offered to convince the rational reader, that man, considered in himself, is a spirit, and that the corporeal part of his composition annexed to him in this natural and material world is in order to his relation thereto, and what he has to do therein, but is not the man himself, but only designed to be instrumental to the operations of his spirit: but, as few are capable of receiving abstract reasonings, and many are apt to run them into matter of doubtful disputation, by arguments drawn from fallacious appearances of sense, I choose, for confirmation of the doctrine in hand, to appeal to truths founded on experience. Such as have confirmed themselves in the belief of the contrary side, are given to think, that, as the beasts have life and sensations as well as men, so they have both the same spirit and the same end; but this is a gross error, as the spirit of a beast immensely differs from that of a man, as being destitute of that sublime principle of a heavenly life, by which the latter is made receptive of the divine influx, and capable of being exalted to a participation of the divine nature; and therefore it is that man is so highly privileged above the beasts, that he can think of God and the things pertaining to

---

*To supposes a human spirit void of a human form and senses, is to annihilate the very idea of spirit; for, as every essence has its proper form, and every form its own essence, (they being necessary correlatives,) so every spirit has its body suited to the world it belongs to, according to that distinction laid down by the apostles: *There is a natural boy, and there is a Spiritual body*, I Cor. xv. 44. And indeed, it is as rational to conclude, that a human spirit should have a human organized body endued with spiritual senses in a spiritual world, as that the same spirit should be invested with a material organized body with natural senses in this natural world. It is to be lamented, and the more for its tendency to promote infidelity, that many of the learned, so called, have in a manner defined and refined spiritual nature into nothing, by divesting it of substantiality, to which it has a more peculiar right by far than matter; nor is the body of an angel less substantial in a proper sense of the word than a solid rock, though not according to the condition of material nature. Upon the whole, the common ideas of the vulgar and illiterate come much nearer to the truth and reality of heavenly things, than the vain conceits of such speculating sciolists.

his kingdom both in heaven and earth, and be led thereby to love the Creator, and to be united to him: now that which is in the capacity of such union is not liable to perish, like that which is not. For there is in every angel and in every man an inmost and supreme degree or part; which more, immediately admits the divine influx from heaven, whereby all that is within man in the inferior degrees are orderly disposed and regulated. This inmost or supreme part of the spirit or soul, may be called the Lord's entrance into angels and men, nay, his very habitation in them; and hereby it is that man is distinguished from the brute animals, which have it not, and is rendered capable of near communications with heaven in the inner man, of believing in the deity, of loving him, and of seeing him: nay, from hence it is that man is a recipient of understanding and wisdom, and also that he is endowed with a rational life, and an heir of immortality: but how or what the Creator operates in this inmost recess or supreme part of man, exceeds the capacity of an angel to comprehend.

When the body of a man is no longer able to perform its natural functions corresponding to the thoughts and affections of his spirit, and which are derived to him from the spiritual world, then he is laid to die; which comes to pass when the lungs and the heart cease their respiratory and contractile motions. Not that man then suffers extinction of life, but only is separated from that corporeal part of his competition which served him for an instrument of usefulness in this world; but he still continues a living man, and that in a proper and literal sense of the expression, inasmuch as man receives his denomination not from his body, but from his spirit, since it is the latter that thinks in him, and that thought with affection essentially constitutes the man; so that, when any man is said to die, it means no more than that he passes from one world into another: and hence it is, that by *death* in the Scripture, according to the internal (Swedenborgian) sense of the word, is signified resurrection, and continuation of life.

There is a very near correspondence betwixt the spirit and respiration, and the motion of the heart (*systole*), betwixt thinking and respiration, and betwixt the affection of love and the heart; so that, when these two motions cease in the body, a separation presently ensues; for these two motions, viz. that which is respiratory in the lungs, and that with is called the systole or contractile power of the heart, are the two bonds of union, which when broken the spirit is left to itself, and the body, being destitute of life from the spirit, becomes cold and putrefies. That so intimate a communication subsists between the human spirit and respiration, and the heart, is, because all the vital motions in this world depend thereon, not only in common, but also in every particular part of the body.

The spirit of a man remains some little time in the body after all signs of life disappear, but not longer than till a total cessation of all power in the heart ensues, which varies according to the nature of the disease he dies of; for the motion of the heart continues long after in some, but not so in others; but, as soon as the total cessation of it happens; the resuscitation of man commences, and this by the sole power of the Lord. By *resuscitation* here is meant the liberation of the spirit of a man from his body, and the introduction of it into the world of spirits, and commonly called resurrection. That the spirit of a man is not separated from his body before all motion and power in the heart entirely ceases, is because the heart corresponds to the affection of love, which is the very life of man, for it is from love that every one derives his vital heat; therefore, so long as this conjunction lasts, so long the correspondence continues, and it is from correspondence that the spirit actuates and communicates life to the body.

That the form of the spirit of a man is a human form, or, in other words, that the spirit is the true-formed man, may be evinced from many arguments; particularly from these; viz. That every angel is in a perfect human form; that every man is a spirit as to his inner man; and that angels in heaven are from the human race. This also more evidently appears from man's being denominated man from his spirit, and not from his body, and because the corporeal form is an adjunct to the spirit after its form, and not contrariwise, the former being but the clothing of the latter. Moreover, the spirit is the sole moving power in man, acting upon and actuating every the most minute part of the body, insomuch that, when any part no longer derives vital influence therefrom, it presently dies. Now, the ruling powers, which govern the body as their subject, are the thought and the will; but these are from the spirit only, nay constitute its very essence. The reason why we do not see any separate spirit, nor yet that of another man whilst in his body, in its human form, with our present organs of sight, is because these organs of vision are material, and therefore only capable of discerning objects of a material nature, whereas spiritual things must be seen by a spiritual eye;* but, when the corporeal sight is extinguished by the death of the body, and the spirit's eye is opened, then spirits appear to one another in their human form, not only in the spiritual world, but they also see the spirits of those who yet live here in the body.

That a human form is proper to a human spirit, follows from man's being created in the form of heaven, and also receptive of all things of a heavenly nature and order, consequently with the faculty of receiving understanding and wisdom; for, whether we express it by the words, "faculty of receiving understanding and wisdom," or "the faculty of receiving heaven," it comes to one and the same thing. So that what has hitherto been said on this subject, may be understood by the rational man, from his view of causes and their effects, of premises and their consequences; but not so by the obstinately irrational, and that for many assignable reasons; but principally, because he is averse to all doctrines which are contrary to the false principles that he has adopted in the room of truths; and he that has thus shut up his mind hath shut the gate of heaven against himself, so that no light from thence can illuminate his rational faculties; and yet that gate might be opened, if his will did not resist. This makes it evident, that they, who are in false thinking from an evil principle, might be possessed of a rational understanding, if they were in a willing disposition for it; and that the reason why they are not so, is because they love the false above the true, as more agreeing with the evil they have adopted, and which they choose to follow. It is to be observed, that to love and to will a thing is the same; for, what a man wills he loves, and what he loves he also wills.

When the spirit of a man enters into the world of spirits, which is soon after his resuscitation, (of which mention has been made before,) he as yet retains the same face and voice that he had in this world, as being hitherto in his exterior state, that of his interior being yet unmanifested; and this is his first state after death; but some time after, his face becomes entirely changed, so as to correspond with the particular affection or love that possessed his spirit when in the body; for the face of a man's spirit differs greatly from that of his body, the latter being derived from his parents, but the former a correspondent to his predominant

---

*It is to be noted here, that, when spirits are seen by any one in the body, they are not seen with the corporeal organs of vision, but by the spirit of the beholder abstractedly from the body, though the appearance is exactly the same in both cases, as implied in those words of the apostle, where, speaking of his visions, he says, *Whether in the body or out of the body, I cannot tell.* 2 Cor. xii. 2.

affection, of which it is the signature or image, and which becomes appropriated to man in the other world, upon the manifestation of his interior state; for the spirit of a man, rightly considered, is the same with his predominant affection or love, and his face is the external form of it. This change respecting faces, in those who pass from hence into the other world, is founded on this law, that no dissimulation or counterfeiting is there allowed, but all must appear to be what they really are, and consequently express their thoughts in their words, and their affections and desires in their looks and actions, so that the faces of all there represent their minds respectively. Hence it is, that, though all who know one another in this world are alike mutually acquainted in the world of spirits, yet it is otherwise in heaven and hell.

The faces of hypocrites undergo not their proper change so soon as the faces of others, and that because they have by custom contracted a habit of forming their minds to a kind of imitation of good sentiments and affections, and therefore they appear not uncomely for some time; but, as the disguise gradually wears off, and their inmost thoughts and affections manifest themselves, they appear more ugly than others. The hypocrites here spoken of, are such as know how to talk like angels upon divine subjects, and yet in their hearts exalt Nature on God's throne, and disbelieve all heavenly truths acknowledged in the Christian church.

It is to be observed, that the human form of every man after death is beautiful in proportion to the love he had for divine truths, and a life according to the same, for by this standard things within receive their outward manifestation and form; so that, the deeper grounded the affection for what is good, the more conformable it is to the divine order in heaven, and consequently the more beauty the face derives from its influx. Hence it is, that the angels of the third or inmost heaven, whose love is of the third or highest degree, are the most beautiful of all the angels; whereas they whose love for divine things had been in a lower degree, or more external than that of the celestial or highest angels, possess an inferior, degree of beauty; and the translucent lustre in their faces, as proceeding from a smaller degree of divine virtue within them, is comparatively dim; for, as all perfection rises in degrees from the inward to the inmost, so the external beauty, to which it gives life and vigour, has its degrees in the same proportion.

When a man passes from this natural world into the spiritual, which is at the time of his death, he takes with him all that belonged to him as a man, and possesses every sense, both external and internal, that he possessed before. Thus, for instance, all in heaven have their sight, their hearing, and all their senses, in far greater perfection than when in this world, and also their minds more abundantly replete with wisdom: for they see by the light of heaven, which greatly exceeds that of this world, and they hear through the medium of a spiritual atmosphere, to which that of our earth is not comparable. The comparative difference between these two senses there and here, is as that of a bright sky to a thick fog, or as the lustre of the meridian sun to the bulk of the evening. Now the light of heaven, which is the divine truth, makes manifest the minutest things to the perception of angels; and, as their external corresponds to their internal or intellectual sight, so by mutual influx they co-operate in forming the high perfection of angelic perspicuity. In like manner their sense of hearing corresponds to their perception, both in the understanding and will; so that, in the sound of the voice, and in the words of the speaker, they can trace the minute particulars of his affections and thoughts; in the sound what relates to his affections, and in the words what concerns his mind or thoughts; but it is to be observed, that the other senses of the angels are not in the same high degree of perfection with those of sight and hearing, and that because the latter are subservient instruments to their understanding and wisdom, and not so the others, which, if equal in power, would lessen their preference to intellectual delights over and above those of their spiritual bodies, as we find to be the case with men in this world, who, according to their greater relish and indulgence as to their grosser senses, have the less appetite and sensibility with respect to spiritual things.

A few words shall here be spoken concerning the cultivation of the rational faculty in man. Genuine rationality consists in truths, not in false-hoods. Now truths are of three kinds; civil, moral, and spiritual. Civil truths relate to judicial matters, and such as respect public government, and, in a general consideration, justice and equity: moral truths have relation to the conduct of life with respect to societies and inferior connections; in general, to sincerity and rectitude; and in particular, to virtues of every class; but spiritual truths relate to the things of heaven and of the church on earth; and in general to the good of love, and the truths of faith. There are three degrees of life in every man: the rational part in man is opened to the first degree by civil truths; to the second by moral truths; and to the third by spiritual truths. But let it here be observed, that man's rational part is not opened and formed merely by his knowing such truths, but by living according to them when known; that is, by loving them with a spiritual affection, or the affection of his spirit, or, in other words, by loving justice and equity as such, sincerity and rectitude of manners as such, and good and truth as such; whereas, to love them only from external regards, is loving them for the sake of self, for one's own character, honour, or profit; and therefore such a love, as it terminates in self, gives not a man any right to the character of rational, as such a one uses truths as a lordly master uses his servants, viz. for his pleasure or interest: and where this is the case, they make no part of the man, nor open so much as the first degree of life in him, but only have a place in his memory, like other scientific ideas, under a material form, where they unite with the love of self in mere animal nature. Hence it may appear how man becomes truly and properly rational, viz. in the third or highest degree, by the spiritual love of good and truth, or the things of heaven, and its representative the church; in the second degree, by the love of sincerity and rectitude; and in the first degree, by the love of justice and equity; which two last loves become spiritual by influx of the spiritual love of good and truth from the highest degree, by joining itself to the inferior loves, and forming in them its own likeness. There are three degrees in man corresponding to the three heavens; and, as the third or highest heaven does, as it were, sanctify the two inferior heavens by the descending influx of its celestial superior virtue, so the spiritual love of all that is good and true in mam (corresponding to the third heaven) spiritualizes or sanctifies his virtues, though of an inferior class; thus, to give a cup of cold water to another is a little thing; but when it is the most we can do, and love is in the doing of it, the act has in it the essence of Christian charity. *Matth.* x. 42.

There are three states which man goes through after death, before he enters into heaven or hell; the first respects his exterior part; the second his interior; and the third is his state of final preparation. These states man passes through in the world of spirits. However there are exceptions, as some are immediately after death taken up into heaven, or cast into hell. Of the former class are they who are regenerated, and so prepared for heaven in this world, and that in so high a degree as to need only the putting off all their natural impurities, in order to be carried by the angels into heaven. On the other hand, such as have been internally evil, under the mask of externally-apparent goodness, and so have filled up the measure of their iniquities by hypocrisy and deceit, using the cloak of goodness as a means whereby to deceive others; these are immediately cast into hell. There are also some who are committed to caverns immediately after their decease, and so separated from others in the world of spirits, but afterwards released, and remanded thither by turns; such are they who, under civil pretexts, deal fraudulently with their neighbours; but the fore-mentioned are very few compared to the many classes of those who are detained in the world of spirits, in order to their preparation for heaven or hell, according to the established order of divine economy.

As to the first state before-mentioned, or that which respects the exterior, this man enters upon immediately after death. Every one's spirit has belonging to it properties exterior and interior: the former are those by which he governs and accommodates the corporeal functions in this world, more especially the face, speech, and bodily gestures, according to his social connections; the latter are proper to his will and free thoughts, which are seldom made manifest by the face, speech, and outward behaviour, man being accustomed through education and example to counterfeit friendship, sincerity, and benevolence, and to conceal his true thoughts, even from his infancy. Hence it is, that so many learn the external practice of morality and good manners, however different they may in reality be within, and so, mistaking custom for principle, know not themselves, nor enter into any examination concerning the matter.

As the life of men newly become spirits is so like to their natural life in this world, and as they are at first strangers to their new state, without knowing any thing more of heaven and hell than what they have learned from the letter of scripture, and their preachers; therefore, after wondering for some time at their being clothed with a body, and possessing every sense as in this world, and also at their seeing things under the like appearance as before, they find themselves urged by a desire of knowing what and where heaven and hell are; upon which they are instructed by their friends in things relating to eternal life, and are conducted to various places, and different societies, and some into cities, gardens, and beautiful plantations, and more, particularly to see magnificent buildings, as such external objects suit with the present external state of their minds. Then they are led to inspect those interior sentiments and ideas, which they had in this life concerning the state of souls after death, and concerning heaven and hell, not without indignation to think of their own past ignorance, and also that of the church, in relation to these important subjects. Almost all in the world of spirits are desirous to know whether they shall go to heaven or not; and the greater part judge in favour of themselves as to this particular, especially such as had lived by the external rules of morality and civil obligation here; not considering that both good and bad do the same to outward appearance, as also do many good offices to others, and in, like manner go to church, hear sermons, and bear a part in the public worship; not reflecting that these external acts and this outward form of worship, avail nothing in themselves, considered separately from the disposition and principle of the worshipper, and that it is the interior of inner man that stamps the character and value upon the outward work and form; but scarcely one in a thousand knows what is meant by the interior, and, even after being taught it, place all in the words and bodily service; and such is the greater part of those who at this day pass from the Christian world into the other.

The second state of man after death is called his interior state, as he then passes into the more recondite things of his mind, or of his will and thoughts whilst the more external functions of it, as exercised in his first state, are then quiescent and dormant. Whoever carefully attends to the lives, words, and actions, of men, may soon find that every one has both his exterior and interior thoughts and intentions; thus, for example, the man of civil connections and manners forms his judgment of others by what he knows of them by character and conversation; and, though he should find them to be far otherwise than men of probity and worth, yet he does not speak and behave to them according to his real sentiments of them, but with something of seeming respect and civility: and this is still more strongly exemplified in the behaviour of persons addicted to dissimulation and flattery, who speak and act quite contrary to what they think and mean; and also in hypocrites, who can talk of God, of heaven, and spiritual things, and also of their country and neighbour, as if from faith and love, when at the same time they have neither the one nor the other, and love none but themselves. This evinces that there are thoughts in the same mind of two different complexions, the one interior, and the other exterior and that it is common for men to speak from the latter, whilst their real sentiments in the interior are contrary thereto; and that these two arrangements of thoughts are of distinct and separate apartments in the mind, appears from the pains such persons take to prevent those that are interior from flowing into the exterior to manifestation. Now man was so formed by his original creation, that both these were as one by correspondence and consent, as is the case now with the good, who both think and speak what is good and true; whereas, in the evil the interior and the exterior are divided, for they think evil, and speak good, thus inverting the order of things, whilst the evil is innermost, and the good outermost, the former exercising rule over the latter, and using its services for temporal and selfish ends; so that the seeming good which they say and do is corrupted and changed into evil, however the undiscerning may be deceived by its outward appearance. On the other hand, they who are in the good principle stand in the divine order of God's creation, whilst the good in their interior flows into the exterior of their minds, and thence into their words and actions. This is the state in which man was created, and thus they have communication with heaven, and have the Lord for their leader. Thus much may serve to show, that man thinks from two distinct grounds, the one called the interior, the other the exterior; and, when we speak here of his thinking, we include likewise his faculty of willing, as his thoughts are from his will, neither can they exist separately.

After that man, now become a spirit, has gone through his first state, which is that of his exterior thoughts and will, he then passes into his second or interior state, and this he enters upon insensibly, which resembles that of a man of this world, who, finding himself at liberty from every restraint and dissipation, recollects himself, and enters into the most secret recesses of his soul. Now in this state of introversion, when he thinks freely from his inmost disposition and affections, he is properly himself, or in his true life. All without exception enter into this state in the other world, as proper to spirit, for the former is assumed and practised in accommodation to society and transactions in this world; and therefore, though it remains with man for some time after death, yet it is not long continued in, as not being suitable to the nature of a spirit, for the following reasons: first, because a spirit thinks and speaks from the governing principle of life without disguise; nay, the same is the case of man in this world, when he enters into his inmost self, and takes an intuitive view of his inward map, in which kind of survey he sees more in a minute than he could utter in an hour. Secondly, because in his conversation and dealings in this world, he speaks and acts under the restraint of those rules which society has established for the maintenance of civility and decorum. Thirdly, because man, when he enters into the interior recesses of his spirit, exercises rule over his outward economy, preferring laws thereto, how to speak and act in order to conciliate the good will and favour of others, and that by a constrained external behaviour. These considerations may serve to show, that this interior state of liberty is not only the proper state of the spirit of a man after death, but even in this life. When a spirit has passed into this second or interior state, it then appears outwardly what manner of man he had been in this world, as he now acts from his proper self; thus, if he had been a wise and good man before, he now manifests still higher degrees of rationality and wisdom in his words and actions, as being freed from those corporeal and earthly embarrassments which had fettered and obscured the inward operations of his mind, whereas the bad man evidences greater folly than before; for, whilst in this world, he fashioned his external behaviour by the rules of prudence, in order to save appearances; but, not being under the like restraints now, he gives full scope to his insanity.

All who in this world lived uprightly, and preserved a good conscience, walking in the fear of God, and in the love of divine truths, applying the same to practical use, seem to themselves as men awaked out of sleep, and as having passed from darkness to light, when they first enter upon their second or interior state; for they think upon the light of pure wisdom, and they do all things from the love of goodness; heaven influences their thoughts and affections, and they are in communication with angels. But the condition of the evil in this state is according to his particular concupiscence. They who had been absorbed in self-love, so as not to attend to the good uses of their respective offices and functions, but discharged them only with a view to their own estimation and honour, appear more stupid than others; for, in proportion to the degree of self-love in any one is his distance from heaven, and consequently from wisdom; but they, who to the evil of self-love had added crafty devices, and by means thereof advanced themselves to worldly honours, associate themselves to the worst of spirits, and addict themselves to the magical arts, which are profane abuses of the divine order, by means of which they molest and vex all that pay them not honour. The practising of insidious wiles, and to kindle strife and hatred, yield them the highest pleasure; they burn with revenge, and long for nothing more than to tyrannise over all that submit not to their will; and all these wicked passions they gratify as far as their evil associates give them assistance; nay, so far does madness hurry them on, as to make them with to scale heaven, either to subvert the government of the holy kingdom, or to cause themselves to be worshipped for gods therein. As to those who in this world ascribed all creation to nature, and so in effect denied a God, and consequently all divine truths, such herd together in this state, calling every one a god who excelled in subtlety of reasoning, and giving him divine-honour. Such in the world of spirits are seen in their conventicle worshipping a magician, holding conferences concerning nature, and behaving more like brute beasts than human creatures; and among them some who were dignitaries in this world, and had the reputation of being learned and wise, and others of a different character. From this much we may gather what they are, the interior of whose minds is shut against divine things, as theirs is, who receive no influx from heaven through looking up to God and a life of faith.

The third state of man, or of his spirit, after death, is the state of instruction, which is appointed for those that go to heaven, and become angels; but not for those that go to hell, as such are not in a capacity of instruction, and therefore their second state is their last, and answers to the third in others, as it terminates in their total change into that prevailing love which constitutes their proper principle, and consequently into a conformity to that infernal society with which they have fellowship. When this is accomplished, their will and thoughts flow spontaneously from their predominant love, which being infernal, they can only choose the evil and false, and reject all that apparent good and truth which before they had adopted, solely as means subservient to the gratification of their ruling passion. On the other hand, the good spirits are introduced from their second into their third state, which is that of preparation for heaven by the means of instruction; for none can be qualified for heaven but through the knowledge of spiritual good and truth, and their opposites, evil and falsehood, which can only come from previous instruction. As to good and truth in a civil and moral sense, commonly called justice and sincerity, these may be learned from the laws of nations, and from conversation in virtuous company; but spiritual good and truth, as ingrafted principles in the heart, are only received by the teachings of a divine light: for, though they are literally set forth in the Scripture, And the doctrines of the Christian churches founded thereon, yet they only gain the efficacy of a vital principle from a celestial influence manifesting itself in a conscientious obedience to the divine laws, as promulgated in the written word, and that in resect to the divine authority of them, and not from selfish and worldly motives; then a man is in the heavenly life, or so heaven, even whilst in this world.

The way of conveying instruction in the other world differs from that on earth, inasmuch as truths there are committed not to the memory, but to the life; for the memory of spirits is in their life's principle, and they receive and imbibe only what is conformable thereto; for spirits are so many human forms of their own affections. As the nature of spirits is such, therefore they are continually inspired with an affection for truth for the uses of life; for the Lord has so ordered it, that every one should love the uses that accord with their particular gifts and qualities: which love is likewise heightened by the hope of their becoming angels; for in heaven all particular and singular uses have relation to the general use or good of the Lord's kingdom, and may be considered as so many parts of one whole, so that the truths which they learn are both truths and the uses of truths conjunctly: thus the angelical spirits are prepared for heaven. The affection or love of truth for the purposes of use is insinuated into them by many ways not known in this world, more particularly by various representations of use under such delightful forms as affect both their minds and senses with unspeakable pleasure; so that, when any spirit is joined to the society for which he was prepared, he then enjoys life most when he is in the exercise of its proper uses. Hence it may appear, that not the ideal knowledge of truths, as things without us, but an implantation of them in the affections and life for the purpose of uses, is that which qualifies for the kingdom of heaven.

After that the angels are duly prepared for heaven in manner described, which comes to pass in a short time, as spiritual minds are of quick comprehension, they are then clothed in angelical garments, which, for the most part, are white, as of fine linen, and conduced to the way which leads up to heaven, and delivered to the guardian angels there; after which they are received by other angels, and introduced to different societies, where they partake of various delights: after this every one is led by the Lord's guidance to his particular proper society, and this by various ways, sometimes direct, sometimes otherwise, not known to any of the angels, but to the Lord only. Lastly, when they are come to their own society, their inmost thoughts and affections open and expand themselves; which meeting with the like returns of cordial sympathy from their fellow-angels, they are immediately known and received by them with a joyful welcome.

An equilibrium is necessary to the existence and subsistence of all things, and consists in the equality of action and reaction between two opposite powers, producing rest or equilibrium; and this according to an established law through the natural world; observed in the very atmospheres, in which the lower and denser air re-acts on the superincumbent columns; nay, even betwixt heat and cold, light and darkness, dry and moist; and the middle point is the temperature or equilibrium. The same law obtains throughout the three great kingdoms of this world, the mineral, vegetable, and animal; wherein all things proceed and are regulated according to action and reaction, or actives and passives, producing or restoring an equilibrium in nature. In the physical world, the agent and re-agent are called power and conatus*; and in the spiritual world, life and will, as being living power and conatus; and here the equilibrium is called liberty. Thus there exists a spiritual equilibrium or liberty betwixt good and evil, by the action of one, and the re-action of the other; for example, in good men this equilibrium is effected by the action of the good principle, and the re-action of the evil principle; but in bad men, evil is the agent, and good is but the re-agent. That there is a spiritual equilibrium betwixt good and evil, is because every thing appertaining to the vital principle in man has relation to good or evil, and the will is the receptacle of both. There is likewise an equilibrium betwixt true and false; but this depends on the equilibrium betwixt good and evil, according to their kinds respectively. The equilibrium betwixt truth and falsehood is similar to that which is betwixt light and darkness *(umbrum)*, which operates, according to the heat and cold therein, on the subjects of the vegetable kingdom; for, that light and darkness have no such operation in themselves alone, but only through the heat in them, may appear from the similarity there is betwixt the light and darkness in winter and in spring. The comparison of truth and falsehood with light and darkness is from correspondency; for truth corresponds to light, and falsehood to darkness, and heat to the good of love. Spiritual light also is the same with truth; and spiritual darkness is the same with falsehood.

There is a perpetual equilibrium betwixt heaven and hell; from the latter continually exhales and ascends a conatus of doing evil; and from the former continually emanes and descends a conatus (tendency to or will) of doing good. In this equilibrium is the world of spirits, which is situated in the midst betwixt heaven and hell; and this may appear from hence, that every man immediately after death enters into the world of spirits, and there continues in the same state in which he died; is examined and proved thereby, as a touchstone of his principles; and remains under the same free will, which all indicate an equilibrium; for, such a spiritual equilibrium there is in every man and spirit, as observed before. The particular kind and tendency of this liberty or free will is well known by the angels in heaven, by the communication of thoughts and affections; and it appears visibly to the evangelical spirits, by the paths and ways

---

*[innate tendency]

which they choose to walk in, as the good spirits take those which lead to heaven, and the evil spirits those which lead to hell; for such ways and walks have actually a visible appearance in that world; and this is the reason that the word *way* or *ways* in Scripture signifies those truths which lead to good, and, in an opposite sense, those false-hoods which lead to evil; and hence also it is, that "to go, walk, or journey," signify the progressions of life in the same sacred writings.

That evil continually inhales and ascends from hell, and that good continually flows and descends from heaven, is because every one is surrounded by a spiritual sphere, flowing or transpiring from his vital affections and thoughts, and consequently the same from every society celestial or infernal, and collectively from the whole heaven and the whole hell. This universal efflux of good from heaven originates in the Lord, and passes through the angels without any mixture of their property or self-hood; for this is suppressed in them by the Lord, who grants them to live in his own divine property; whereas the infernal spirits are in their property of selfish nature, or what only belongs to themselves, which, as unblessed with divine communications from the sole fountain of all good, is only evil in every one continually.

The heavens, in the general; are distinguished into two kingdoms; the one of which is called the celestial, the other the spiritual kingdom. The hells likewise are distinguished into two kingdoms; the one of which is opposite to the celestial, the other to the spiritual. That which is opposite to the celestial is in the west, and they who belong to it are called genii; and that; which is opposite to the spiritual kingdom is in the north and south, and they who belong to it are called evil spirits. All in the celestial kingdom, excel in love to the Lord, and all that are in the hells opposite to that kingdom are under the prevailing power of self-love; all that belong to the spiritual kingdom are distinguished in excellence by love to their neighbour, and all that are in the hells opposite to this kingdom are slaves to the love of the world; so that love to the Lord and the love of self are in the same diametrical opposition to each other as the love of our, neighbour and the love of the world. Effectual provision is made by the Lord, that no power of evil, from the hells that are in opposition to the celestial kingdom, may reach the subjects of the spiritual kingdom, as the consequence in that case would be the subversion of the latter. Thus does the Lord keep the balance betwixt good and evil in his own hand for the preservation of his kingdoms.

As good and evil, truth, and falsehood, are of a spiritual nature, so also is that equilibrium in which consists the power of thinking and willing the one or the other, and the liberty of choosing or refusing accordingly. This liberty, or freedom of the will, originates in the divine nature, but is given to every man by the Lord for a property of his life, nor does he ever take it back again. This good gift to man is to the end that he may be regenerated, and saved, for without free will there is no salvation for him; but that he actually possesses it, he may know from the operations of his own mind, and what passes inwardly in his spirit, he being able to think and choose either good or evil, whatever restraints he may be under from uttering or acting the latter part in respect to laws divine or human. Now this inward experience evinces, beyond a thousand arguments, that liberty belongs to man, as his spirit is his proper self, and it is that which freely thinks, wills, and chooses; consequently, liberty is to be estimated according to the inner man, and not from what he may be outwardly through fear, human respects; or other external restraints.

That man would not be capable of being reformed or regenerated without free will, is because he is by the original constitution of his nature born to evils of every kind, which must be removed in order to his salvation; and that can only be by his knowing, owning, renouncing, and abhorring them...To this end, he must be instructed in the nature of good; for it is by good only that he can see the evil, but by evil he cannot see the good: accordingly, he must be early educated in the knowledge of spiritual truths, by teaching, by reading the scriptures, and by the preaching of the word, that so he may attain to the right understanding of what is good; as he is likewise to cultivate his mind with the knowledge of moral and civil truths from his intercourse with society in the different relations of life; all which imply the use and exercise of freedom. Another thing to be considered is, that nothing becomes appropriated to man, or can be called his own, that is not received into the affectionate part; other things he may apprehend or form an ideal knowledge of, but what enters not his will or love, which is the same thing, (for what a man wills he loves,) that makes no part of him, nor abides with him. Now, man being naturally prone to evil, he could not receive its contrary, the good, into his will or love; so as to become appropriated to him, unless he were endowed with liberty or freedom of will, seeing that the good is opposite to the evil of his nature.

As man is possessed of liberty or free will, in order to be capable of regeneration, therefore he can have communication in spirit with heaven or with hell; for evil spirits from the one, and angels from the other, are present with him; by the former he possesses his own evil; by the latter he is in the principle of good from the Lord; and herein stands his equilibrium or liberty. Not that this conjunction of man with heaven or hell is an immediate conjunction, but mediate only, and that through the spirits that belong to the world of spirits; for these are the spirits that attend on man, and not any immediately from heaven or hell. By the evil spirits belonging to the world of spirits, man joins himself to hell; and by the good spirits of the same world he has communication with heaven; for the world of spirits is intermediate between heaven and hell, and constitutes the true equilibrium. Let it be observed, as touching those spirits that are appointed to be man's associates here, that a whole society may hold communication with another society, and also with any individual wheresoever, by means of an emissary spirit, which spirit is called, *The subject of many*. The case is similar with respect to man's communication with the societies in heaven and in hell, by the intervention of his associate spirit from the world of spirits. The good spirits belonging to the world of spirits, being in their final preparation for the angelical state, are called angelical spirits; and, as they have immediate communication with the heavenly angels, so has man, through them, a mediate communication with the same. And the bad spirits *vice versa*. Thus all communications, between man and the highest and lowest in heaven and hell, are conducted through the mediums adapted to his nature and states respectively.

What has been delivered concerning heaven, the world of spirits, and hell, will appear obscure to those who have no relish for spiritual truths, but clear to such as take delight therein, more especially to all who are in the love of truth for its own sake. What we love, we readily receive and understand; and, where truth is the object of our affections, it recommends itself to the mind by the evidence it brings with it; for truth is the light, by which all things are known and distinguished.

Such are the doctrines of Baron Emanuel Swedenborg, with respect to the spirits and departed souls of men. But the *Magi* or wise men of the East, have defined spirits, good and bad, of a great variety of kinds and orders, whereof some are suited to the purposes of witchcraft and exorcism, and others not. The form and nature of spirits, say they, are to be considered according to the source to which each *caterva** doth belong; for

*[troupe]

some, being altogether of a divine and celestial nature, are not subject to the abominable conjurations and enchantments of vicious men; whilst others, of a diabolical and infernal nature, are not only ready upon all occasions to become subservient to exorcists and magicians, but are ever watching opportunities of exciting evil affections in the mind, and of stirring up the wickedly-inclined to the commission of every species of iniquity and vice. As to the shapes and various likenesses of these wicked spirits or devils, it is generally believed, that, according to their different capacities in wickedness, so their shapes are answerable after a magical manner, resembling spiritually some horrid and ugly monsters, as their conspiracies against the power of God were high and monstrous when they fell from heaven. For the condition of some of them is nothing but continual horror and despair, whilst others triumph in fiery might and pomp, attempting to pluck the Almighty from his throne; but the quality of heaven is shut from them, and they can never reach it, which acts upon them as an eternal source of torment and misery. But that they are *materially* vexed and scorched in flames of fire, is only a figurative idea, adapted to our external sense, and by no means to be literally understood; for their substance is spiritual, and their essence too subtile for any external torment. Their misery is unquestionably great and infinite; but not through the effect of outward flames; for their bodies are capable of piercing through wood and iron, stone and all terrestrial things. Neither is all the fire or fuel of this world able to torment them; for in a moment they can pierce it through and through. The endless source of their misery is in themselves, and stands continually before them, so that they can never enjoy any rest, being absent from the presence of God; which torment is greater to them than all the tortures of this world combined together.

The wicked souls that are departed this life, are also capable of appearing again, and of answering the conjurations and magical questions of exorcists, because the quality of their minds, and the bent of their inclination, being similar to those of the fallen angels or devils, it cannot be conceived that their torment and pursuits hereafter are much different; for the Scripture saith, *that every one is rewarded according to his works;* and, *that which a man sows, that he shall reap*. Hence it follows, that, as the damned spirits of departed men, while they lived on earth, heaped up vanity, and loaded their souls with iniquity and vice; so, when they enter the next world, the same abominations which here they committed serve them to ruminate and feed upon, and, the greater these offences have been, the greater is the torment arising from them every moment. But very contrary to this is the fate of the righteous souls, departed, who are entered into eternal rest; and of the different degrees and orders of the angelic host, which appertain to heaven, and have places in the mansions of the blessed. Nor is it possible for any one, how expert soever in magical experiments, to compel these blessed spirits, of any degree, order, or quality, of creation, to be exorcised, or called up, or made appear, *at the will of the magician*, by any forms of convocation or communication, or by the power of magical rites and ceremonies of any class or description whatsoever. It may indeed be believed, and it is by most authors admitted, that infinite numbers of the angelic host are employed for the glory of God, in watching over and protecting the pursuits of good men; but they are not subject to spells or conjurations of any kind set on foot by the impious professors of the Black Art.

Of a different opinion, however, are some of those who attempt to justify the magic art under sanction of the holy Scriptures, and for this purpose instance the supplication of Saul to the witch of Endor. This passage undoubtedly serves to show how greatly the practice of exorcism reigned amongst the Jews, and proves the possibility of raising up spirits in those ancient times; but that the exorcist never meant to bring up the spirit or ghost of Samuel, but that of an evil daemon to represent him, is apparent from her exclamations to Saul, when she accuses him of having deceived her; and is a convincing proof, that this particular instance, of the similitude of a blessed spirit being called up by a professor of spells and incantations, was owing to the immediate permission of the Deity, for the purposes of forwarding the Jewish dispensation, and manifesting his peculiar regard to the person of David, through whose loins the Messiah was to come. See I Sam. xxviii. 7, & seq.

Such spirits as are termed *astral spirits*, which belong to this outward world, and are compounded of the elemental quality, having their source from the stars, and being subject to a beginning and ending, may be solicited and brought into league with magicians and witches; and can also inform them of many wonderful and occult properties in nature, and of many important concerns relating to the state and affairs of men in this terrestrial world. This description of spirits is said to occupy various places of the earth; as woods, mountains, waters, air, fiery flames, clouds, stars, mines, sea-shores, ancient buildings and ruins, and places of the slain. They are capable of hunger, grief, passion, and vexation, being in some measure temporal, and compounded of the most spiritual part of the elements, into which they are eventually resolved, as ice into water; and have been more or less celebrated by historians and poets in all ages of the world.

There are likewise another species, called Igneous or Fiery Spirits, that inhabit the burning mountains of Hecla, Vesuvius, AEtna, Poconzi, &c. which some authors have affirmed to be *infernal* Spirits, and damned souls, who for a term of years are confined to these burning mountains for their iniquities. But the most received opinion is, that they are of a middle, vegetative nature, and perishable, which, at the dissolution of the *media natura*[*], shall be again reduced into their primary aether. And from natural causes it may be easily demonstrated, that there is great correspondence betwixt such substances and the element of fire, by reason of the internal flagrat and central life proceeding from the quintessence of one only element, which upholds them in motion, life, and nourishment; as every natural and supernatural being is upheld and maintained out of the self-same root from whence it had its original. So the angels feed upon the celestial manna; the devils upon the fruits of hell, which is natural to the *propensity* of their appetites; the astral spirits upon the source of the stars, and the gas of the air; upon a principle that every thing is nourished by its mother, as infants at the breast, or chickens from the egg, &c. The proper nourishment of fiery spirits, however, is radical heat, and the influence of the airy region; nor is it to be wondered at that they are so much delighted with the fiery quality, in regard of their affinity and near approach to the essence and quality of infernal spirits or devils, whose state and being is altogether damnable and deplorable; for, although they have not the ability of attaining either the heavenly or infernal quality, by reason that they are utterly void of the innermost centre, and may be rather termed monsters than rational animals; yet, because they are compounded of the outermost principle, such is their innate affinity and unity with the dark world, or infernal kingdom, that they often become the devil's agents, to propagate his works upon the face of the earth. Thus by the instigation of infernal spirits, and their own promptitude, they often terrify men with nocturnal visions; provoke melancholy people to suicide; tempt drunkards and incendiaries to set houses on fire, to burn those who are in them, and allure careless servants and others to sound and incautious sleep, that such unlucky accidents might happen; besides innumerable other ways they have of executing the devices of iniquitous spirits through malicious instigations, or secret stratagems, projected for

---

* [middle nature]

the overthrow and destruction of mortal men; especially when the work to be effected by the devil is too hard for his subtle and spiritual nature to effect, because the same belongs to the outward source or principle to which these dubious spirits more immediately belong. For, being compounded of the fiery element, they are most officious in this kind of service, being such as the antecedent matter hath sufficiently demonstrated; but according to their different ranks and orders some of them are much more inveterate and malicious in their agency than the rest. These, as well as every other kind of astral spirits, are more or less obsequious to the kingdom of darkness; and the devil, it seems, can effect little or nothing without their assistance in this outward or elementary world, upon the passions of mankind; because their bodies are too crude for the direct conveyance of their influence, either in dreams, charms, visions, raptures, or other soft and alluring means. These fiery spirits are likewise apt for conjuration, and are always ready at the call of the magician, for the execution of any cruel or diabolical purpose

Distinct from fiery spirits, are a species which properly belong to the metallic kingdom, abiding in mountains, caves, dens, deeps, hiatas or chasms of the earth, hovering over hidden gold, tombs, vaults, and sepultures of the dead. These spirits are termed by the ancient philosophers "protectors of hidden treasure," from a principle or quality in their nature, whence they exceedingly delight in mines of gold, silver, and places of hidden treasure; but are violently inimical to man, and envy his benefit or accommodation in the discovery thereof; ever haunting those places where money is concealed, and retaining malevolent and poisonous influences to blast the lives and limbs of those who attempt to make such discoveries; and therefore extremely dangerous for magicians to exorcise or call them up. It is recorded in several of the ancient British authors, that Peters, the celebrated magician of Devonshire, together with his associates, having exorcised one of these malicious spirits to conduct them to a subterranean vault, where a considerable quantity of treasure was known to be hid, they had no sooner quitted the magic circle, than they were instantaneously crushed into atoms, as it were in the twinkling of an eye. And in this particular we have too many fatal examples upon record, of the sudden destruction of those who by magical spells had called up this description of spirits, for the purpose of discovering hidden gold; which examples seem to prove, that these spirits have more affinity with the infernal than with the astral hierarchy; and that they are the diabolical agents of Mammon, bringing about all the evils of this world, which spring from an insatiable lust after gold; whence the saying in scripture, that *We cannot serve God and Mammon;* and that *It is easier for a camel to pass through the eye of a needle, than for a rich man to enter into the kingdom of heaven*; hyperbolically spoken, in reference to the innumerable sins and wickednesses committed by mankind, for the sake of temporary wealth and riches! Hence too a reasons offers, why of all other subordinate spirits, these are the most pernicious to mortal men. The nature of them is so violent, that, in the histories of the gold and silver mines abroad, it is recorded that whole companies of labourers have been destroyed by them at once; and that their delight is in tormenting, killing, and crushing to death, those who most greedily lust after and seek for such treasures. The richest and largest silver-mine in Germany was haunted by one of these spirits, who sometimes used to appear in the shape of a he-goat, with golden horns, pushing down the workmen with uncommon violence; and at others in the shape of a horse, breathing fiery flames and pestilential vapours at his nostrils, till by continual destruction, fear, and alarm, they were obliged to desist from working that mine any longer; and it continues shut to this day.

Thus far we have considered spirits *subordinate*, or such as properly belong to the elementary or outward world. We will now take a view of the infernal spirits or devils, and damned souls; which are to be classed according to their respective ranks and orders, exactly correspondent or apposite to the choirs and hierarchies of the angels, or blessed spirits in heaven.

The origin of devils and infernal spirits, as Scripture-revelation hath confirmed and established, proceeded from conspiracy and rebellion in heaven, under the arch-fiend Lucifer, who was originally of the highest order of the angelic host; because it is written of him, *In Cherubim extentus protegeus posuite monte sancto Dei;* "Extended upon a Cherubim and protecting, I have put thee in the holy mountain of God." And further, because it is also written, *Quomodo enim mane oriebaris, Lucifer;* "For then didst thou rise in the morning, O Lucifer." Various are the opinions as to the express occasion of his fall. Some say, it was for speaking these words: *Ponem sedem meam in aquilone, similis ero Altissimo;* "I will put my feat in the North, and I will be like the Most-High." Others affirm, that it proceeded from his *utterly refusing felicity, and holding the blessings of heaven in derision.* Some again, *because he asserted that all his strength proceeded from himself and not from God.* Others, *because he attempted to effect that by himself and his own strength, which was alone the proper gift of God*. Other opinions say, *That his condemnation proceeded from his challenging the place of the Messiah;* whilst others insist, that it was because he *impiously challenged the omnipotency of God, with whom he claimed equal power*. But the Christian church in all countries agree, that it was for all these crimes put together, and many more; exclusive of his drawing aside the allegiance of other angels, and suborning the whole of his own legion in conspiracy, to attempt to pluck the Almighty from his Throne; whereupon a dreadful conflict ensued between Michael the archangel with the heavenly host on one side and Lucifer and his rebellious tribes on the other, which ended in their total extermination from the mansions and light of heaven, to suffer eternal torment in the dark abodes of the infernal regions.

Here began the kingdom of darkness, and the devil's enmity to mortal man; who being created of a nature inferior to the angels, but, by a state of probation, capable of arriving to the same degree of excellence, and of filling up the vacancy in heaven occasioned by the fall of Lucifer and his legions, it excited his envy still the more, and laid the ground of that ceaseless warfare, which, from the fall of Adam to the present hour, hath existed between the king of darkness and the souls of men. And, though this conflict is not conducted by outward and visible means, yet it is effected by secret snares and ambuscades, which take us at unawares, and when we are most off our guard. For the devil, while we feed, allures us to sin by gluttony; he thrusteth lust into our generation, and sloth into our exercise; into our conversation, envy; into our traffic, avarice; into our correction, wrath; into our government, pride; he putteth into our hearts evil cogitations; and into our mouths, lies. When we awake, he moveth us to evil works; when we sleep, to evil and filthy dreams; he provokes the jocund to lasciviousness, and the sad to despair; whence spring the various evils with which frail human nature is surrounded; and which nothing, but a full confidence in heaven and the gospel-dispensation, can alleviate or remove.

But as to the locality or circumscription of the kingdom of darkness, it is far otherwise to be considered than the common and vulgar idea of it, which esteems the infernal habitation as a distinct chasm or gulph in a certain place, either above, under, or in the centre of, the earth, where innumerable devils and wicked souls inhabit, and are perpetually scorched and tormented with *material* flames of fire. This is the opinion which the vulgar are naturally addicted and prone to believe; But, if we rightly consider the kingdoms of heaven and hell, in respect of each other, we must look upon the similitude of *light* and *darkness* in this outward world, which is not circumscribed, nor separate, as to locality, from one another; for, when the Sun rises, the darkness of the night disappears; not that it removes itself to some other place or country, but the brightness of the light overpowers and swallows it up, so that, though it disappears, yet it is as absolutely there as the light itself. The same similitude is also to be considered in the description of the habitations of good evil beings, that are really in one another, yet not comprehended of one another; neither indeed can they be; for the evil spirits, though they should remove ten thousand miles; yet are they in the same quality and source, never able to find out or discover where the kingdom of heaven is, though it be really through and through *with* the dark kingdom; but in another opposite quality, which separates and makes them eternal strangers to each other. A similitude hereof we have in the faculties of human life considered with respect to the endowments of the soul in the just, and in the wicked; for to be good, pure, and holy, is really present as a quality in *potentia* with the depraved soul, although at that instant the soul be clothed with abomination, so that the eye which should behold God, or goodness, is put out. Yet, if the soul would but come out of itself, and enter into another source, or principle, it might come to see the kingdom of heaven within itself, according to the Scripture and Moses, *The word is nigh there, in thy heart, and in thy mouth*. Deut. xxx. 14. Rom. x. 8.

True it is that the devils, or fallen angels, cannot all alike manifest themselves in this astral world; because the nature of some of them approaches nearer to the external quality than others; so that, although *properly* the very innermost and outermost darkness be their proximate abode, yet they frequently flourish, live, move, and germinate, in the airy region. But, according to the fiery nature, it is very difficult for them to appear in this outward world, because there is a whole principle or gulf betwixt them, namely, they are shut up in another quality or existence, so that they can with greater difficulty find out the being of this world, or come with full pretence unto it, than we can remove into the kingdom of heaven or hell with our intellectual man. For, if it were otherwise, and the devils had power to appear unto mortals as they list, how many towns, cities, &c. would be destroyed, and burnt to the ground! how many infants would be pluckt away in their innocency, and unoffending creatures be destroyed by their malicious powers. Indeed few or none would escape with their lives, or possessions, or sound minds; whereas now all these enjoyments are free amongst mankind; which proves that it is extremely hard for infernal spirits to appear in the third principle of this world; and as difficult as for a man to live under water, or fishes on the shore. Yet we must grant, that, when the imaginations and earnest desires of the wicked have stirred up the centre of hell within themselves, then the devil hath access to this world in their desires, and continues here to vex and torment them, so long as the strength of those desires remain, which was the first attractive cause.

The cause of the paucity of appearances of evil spirits in these days, is the fulness of time, and the brightness of Christianity, dispelling the mists of heresy and idolatry, as the Sun doth the fogs, which vanish on its appearance; not by any violence or compulsion, but from a cause implanted in the nature of things and their opposites. Even so the kingdom of light, as it overspreads the soul in power and dominion, closes up the centre of darkness, and scatters the influences of the devil before it, who becomes as it were entirely *passive* as to the works and will of man. In the time of the law, when the wrath and jealousy of the Father had the dominion in the kingdom of nature, infernal spirits had more easy access to mankind than they now have; for, before the incarnation of Christ, the anger of God was unappeased, and had more dominion over the soul of man, which was then at greater distance from the divine goodness; consequently the devils could with more facility spring up in the elements of wrath, and manifest themselves in this outward principle; because the very idea and basis of hell is founded on the wrath of God, which is the only channel by which the devil is conveyed into this world. So, when the miracles of Christ began to manifest themselves in the world, the multiplicity of diabolical appearances, and possessed with the devil, began insensibly to decay and vanish. It is true, that the greatest instances known of the temptations and power of Satan, were exercised in that space of time betwixt the incarnation and crucifixion of our Saviour; yet it is as certain, that the devil knew he had but a short time longer to uphold his kingdom here, and therefore he employed all his strength and forces to torment those captive and miserable souls to whom Christ came to preach deliverance. But, after the partition wall was broken down, and the vail of Moses, and the wrath of God, were removed, there was a sensible and visible decay of Satan's power in the world; so that, though it be possible, even in these days, by a renunciation of the salvation of Christ, and by becoming a disciple of the devil, to hold correspondence, with, or to be wholly possessed by, him; yet these things happen so rarely, and require so depraved a state of mind and conduct, that whenever they are pretended so to be, there is great room to doubt the truth of such assertions, though *apparently* well authenticated.

But, notwithstanding that the coming of Christ has thus curtailed the power of the devil over all Christian countries, yet such nations as have never embraced the Christian faith, but pursue the ancient superstition and idolatry, are still deluded and bewitched by him, because the centre of truth and light never having been awakened in them, the power of Satan easily prevails to seduce them to worship things visible, instead of the true God: for where most darkness and superstition is found, whether in religion or personal understanding, there his power is always most predominant. Thus it is now with the miserable inhabitants of the greatest part of Asia, and the uncultivated and ferocious parts of Africa and America; yet we have hopes that the goodness of providence, in his own fit and appointed season, will, through some favourable channel, communicate the light of the Gospel to those miserable beings, whereby the shocking idea of feeding on human flesh, of devoting one another to destruction and slavery, and of pursuing the insinuations and works of the devil, may be totally abolished, and every part of the habitable globe be united in the acknowledgement of one God, of one Saviour, and of one liberal, candid, and impartial, Christian persuasion.

As to the different shapes and forms of the devils, it is suggested by Scripture, and admitted by all writers upon the subject, that they were answerable in monstrosity and hideousness to the superior rank they held in heaven, and to the enormity of the offence which was the cause of their fall. Thus, in Revelation, Lucifer, as the leader and prime apostate, is termed the *great dragon*, and king of the devils. And hence it is conceived, that those who belonged to the supreme hierarchies in heaven, and were the foremost to rebel, were, immediately on their expulsion from the realms of bliss, transformed from angels of splendour and glory to devils in the shape of dragons, crocodiles, serpents, tigers, and the like; so that the most perverse and potent among the devils possess the most ugly and frightful of the bestial shapes, but a thousand times more terrific and frightful than can possibly be conceived from the most ferocious of those animals. In this consideration, however, there is a material distinction to be made between the apostate angels and the damned souls, which have deserted God in this world, and become inhabitants of the infernal regions in the other. For the most part, these unhappy creatures retain the human shape, but with aspects dismal and melancholy, and expressive of the unspeakable torments they are doomed to suffer; for in themselves they rest not, neither are they capable of the shortness or duration of time, nor of the alternate courses of day and night. The sins and wickedness they committed in this life is the source of their continual torment, which gnaws and corrodes them, rising and boiling up continually in their minds, without rest or intermission. All the refrigeration they have, is by intercourse with the devils, when the height of wickedness stirs them up to blasphemies against God, and towering up above heaven and omnipotence in their adulterated and deluded imaginations, which, figuratively speaking, serves as sport and pastime amongst one another, but of a short and certain duration. Not that this is of the smallest advantage, or the least mitigation of their torments; for pain discontinued returns the greater; neither would vexation be vexation, if it had no respite nor forbearance, that the contrary might be also manifest, *nam contraria juxta se posita a majus elucescunt*[*]. Yet is their torment exceedingly different; so that the suffering of one in respect to that of another is but a mere dream or phantasy. I mean, amongst the damned souls, and not the devils; for the pain and torment of the devils is greater than the greatest of the lost souls by many million degrees, according to the course of nature and reason; for that which falls highest suffers most, and *optima corrupta fiunt pessima*[†].

But wonderful and manifest are the torments which lost souls endure, according to the various lusts and licentiousness they indulged in whilst they lived upon earth, or died in without expiation or repentance. The cruel murderers, who died in the boiling source of blood and envy, suffer the greatest torment, because they are continually murdering in their imaginations, and seeking, like dreaming men, to effect what the want of the correspondent organ will not permit them to do. For, according to Scripture, and the wisest authors upon this subject, the principal torment and misery of damned souls proceeds from their continually wishing and willing; whence they generate ideas and representations founded on impossibility, which is the source of their continual aggravation, disappointment, and misery. By the same reasoning, those who died in lust and gluttony, lasciviousness and inebriety, are overwhelmed with correspondent torments, though much inferior to the first. They are continually imagining their former pleasures in the *magia* as in a dream, which, when they awake, torments them cruelly; as with us when we awake from a frightful dream, and find it is only a dream, our pleasure is more susceptible—whereas, with them, the case is reversed; for, as their

---

*[for contraries placed near each other, makes them shine greater]
†[the best when corrupted become the worst]

time is spent in eternal torment, so their dreams of bliss, when they awake, or become more sensible to their misery, but aggravate their misfortunes, and give fresh poignancy to the torments they endure. Such souls, in whom the boiling source of anger and revenge hath had a dwelling or receptacle here, if they depart this life in their sins, do likewise endure a most dreadful kind of torment, which arises continually as a biting worm and hungry fire, to double and accumulate an excess of despair upon them. Those also who reigned in pride and ostentation upon earth, treading under foot the meek and humble in heart, are tortured with the utmost reverie of their desires, which are ever uppermost in their infatuated imaginations. They are ever seeking to pull the Almighty from his throne, and towering up in the pride of their hearts, hoping to gain the kingdom of heaven to insult and boast in. But the quality of the beatific source is utterly occult and estranged from them, so that they can never find, taste, hear, nor see, it, though it be wrapt round and round with their own peculiar source and principle. This adds eternally to their misery, and rises upon their senses with horrible pangs and bitter gnawings, like the irksome and vexatious pains and aches of man's body, only a thousand times more acute and insupportable. The nature also of their habitation is such, that their punishment is exceedingly aggravated that way; because the extremity of the four elements is there converted into a whole principle of wrath and torment. The excess of cold and heat, drought and moisture, are alternately raging amongst them by intercourse; nor is there any light or lustre within their courts, but that which is emitted from their fiery eyes, or flaming nostrils, as a deadly glance or glimmering, which serves only to render the momentary sight of their miserable habitation ten times more disgusting and intolerable. And, as every kind of being feeds upon something proper to his own nature or element, whether it be plant, animal, or metallic production, so the devils are neither destitute of meat nor drink, according to their own kingdom and quality, having fruits springing up, and growing before them, of hellish, sour, and poisonous, natures, which are real and palpable to them, and not imaginary or typical, though to us magical and invisible. Neither is this at all to be wondered at, if we consider the nature of man's soul in *media natura*[*]; for, if it feed not upon the internal and substantial Word, which is the very head of life itself, it must and will of necessity ruminate on something else, viz. the fruits of iniquity; which it takes in and swallows up, even as an ox drinks the water; so that to the soul the sin becomes palpable, glutting, and satiating, from which it never can be freed but by works of expiation

---

[*]   [middle nature]

and repentance. Also, in the astral source, when called up by magical spells and incantations, or otherwise, they are not destitute of food, but receive the influences of the air and water into their *limbus**, which they convert into food, according to their own poisonous quality; as of sweet and wholesome herbs the filthy toads and other venomous reptiles form their poison, converting them into a nature like their own. And so likewise these infernal spirits, considered in respect of the four elements, have a tone or language peculiar to themselves, which they exercise and speak one amongst another, as mortals do; but they have utterly lost the dignity of their sounds according to the eternal nature, and are totally corrupted in their pronunciation or dialect, since they fell from their first celestial glory; so that their articulation is harsh, doleful, fierce, and terrible, like the fruits they feed upon, and place they dwell in. This deprivation is very apparent in the kingdom of this world, in the divided languages of every region, according to the constellation under which they are situated; the true and magical language of nature, notwithstanding the industrious lexicographers, still remaining hidden from the knowledge of every country in the habitable world.

Thus far I have endeavoured to illustrate the causes, natures, and punishments, of infernal spirits; which, notwithstanding, is a subject so intricate and copious in itself, by reason of the variety of their qualities in the source of darkness, wherein they live, move, eat, breathe, and inhabit, having qualities, actions, and passions, innumerable, and which are to mankind almost utterly unknown and incomprehensible,—that to attempt an ample demonstration of the matter, would require deeper speculation than the subject deserves, or than I am master of; particularly as the inhabitants of that gloomy kingdom are never in one regular stay, continuance, or property; but from one hour to another are continually floating and changing, like the swiftness of the winds, or the gliding along of running waters, which pass away as a thought, and are no more remembered. So it is with the devils and damned spirits in that lachrymable state of darkness, where their existence is a continual anguish and torment, shifting from the pangs of one sorrow to the bitterness of another, unto all eternity!

Now according to the spirit of Christian Revelation, there hath been always opposed to the machinations of the devil and his imps upon earth, who *go about like roaring lions seeking whom they may devour*, a certain description of good and holy spirits; whose province it is to watch over the

*   [border, edge]

affairs of men, and to guard them from the invisible assaults of the devil; exclusive of the ministration of God's holy angels, which hath been manifested in a thousand different instances in Scripture, but whose appearances and manifestations to the eyes of mortal man never have been nor can be permitted but on the most important dispensations of divine Providence. The received opinion however is, as to the former doctrine, that there is, according to the disposition of the mind or soul, a good or evil *Genius*, that accompanies invisibly every person born into the world. Their office is principally that of forewarning the persons they attend of any imminent impending danger, sometimes by inward instinct, or by outward appearances; and sometimes by dreams in the night. These *Genii* change their quality and office as the person or party change their's; if from good we degenerate to evil, then by degrees the good genius is estranged from us, and an evil demon naturally succeeds, according to that sympathy of things, wherein each draws after it that which is its like. There have been likewise defined, by the learned doctors and rabbis, who have written on this intricate subject, *seven good Angels*, who watch over and superintend the general affairs of mankind, and who are ever ready to forward, by intellectual association, mental instigation, or strong nocturnal visionary manifestation, the general prosperity and success of all men's affairs who are governed by the laws of integrity and religion, and who are, by some one or other of these means, allured or prompted to such particular conduct or determination as shall tend ultimately to their honour and preferment, to the good of society, and to the glory of God and true religion, which is the grand office of these seven good spirits to promote. And opposed to these are *seven evil Spirits, or Demons*, proper to the infernal world, whose office is to infuse evil into those men's minds who are naturally so addicted, and who never fail to join in association, though invisibly, with depraved persons of every description, whose passions they influence, and whose desires they lead to the commission of all the abominations of this world. The names of the seven good angels or sprits are, 1. *Jubanladace* distinguished in the dominion of thrones, as the appointed guardian of all public and national enterprises, where the good of society, and the honour of God, are unitedly concerned. He is delineated in all the brightness of a celestial messenger, bearing a flaming sword, girded about the loins, with an helmet on his head; and this is the magical character by which he is distinguished, and which is worn by many, as a lamin round the neck, for preservative against putrid infection and sudden death.

The second is *Pah-li-Pah*, one of the celestial powers whose peculiar office it is to guard and forewarn such as are virgins and uncontaminated youth against all the evils of debauchery and prostitution; and to elevate the mind to a love of virtue, honour, and revealed religion. He personifies the character of an illustrious angel, of a bright but most complacent countenance; and is known by the following magical symbol, which is worn about the neck of virgins as a protection from all the assaults of evil demons, and it is said to be infallible against the powers of seduction.

The third is *Nal-gah*, devoted to the protection of those who are assaulted by evil sprits or witches, and whose minds are sunk by fearful and melancholy apprehensions of the assaults of the devil, and the power of death. His proper office is to fortify the mind, and to lead the senses to a contemplation of the attributes of God, and the joys of heaven, the reward of all good works. His appearance is represented as perfectly celestial, having a crown of gold upon his head, with a shield and spear in his hands, for the protection of those over whom he presides. The following is his magical character, which is worn round the neck as a preservation against witchcraft and suicide.

The fourth is *Maynom,* one of the powers who hath the ability of subservient administration and protection; that is, at one and the same time to be present with many. His presence must be sought by humility and prayer. The fifth good Genius is *Gaonim,* an angel of celestial brightness, who hath the peculiar ability of rendering his pupil invisible to any evil spirits whatsoever, as often as attacked by them. The sixth is *Halanu,* the guardian and promoter of all good and great ideas, by whom Bezeliah and Aholiab were divinely inspired for the structure of the tabernacle. The seventh is *Ramah-umi,* the genius of geometrical proportion, and the power of numbers; the secrets and extent of which are not yet half known, even to the most favoured of those whose capacities are enlightened by his superior aid.

Now the office of the seven evil demons or spirits is to counteract and destroy the effect of the good; for, as the power and capacity of the good proceeds from the omnipotence of God in the quality of heaven, so is the force of the *evil Genii,* in the infernal quality, made correspondent thereto, from a principle of contraries; for it is to be noted that these seven *evil* angels, before their fall, enjoyed the same places and degrees of glory, that now belong to the seven *good* angels or Genii; so that, as their office is to instruct and allure mankind to the pursuit of every thing that is good, great, virtuous, and honourable, it is the business of the others to tempt and seduce the mind to a pursuit of whatever is vile, vicious, and abominable, and that may be instrumental in extending the kingdom of darkness and the power of the devil. The names of these seven evil spirits or Genii stand upon record as follow: 1. *Panalcarp,* in the likeness of a crocodile with two heads. 2. *Baratron,* appearing like a magician in a solemn priestly habit. 3. *Sondennah,* in the caparison and similitude of an Indian huntsman. 4. *Greizmodal,* in the fawning shape of a large spaniel dog. 5.*Ballifargon,* in the similitude of a covetous miser, lusting after gold; he is the grand enticer to thieving and robbery, and usually brings his followers to an ignominious and destructive end. 6. *Morborgran,* who, under various likenesses of a friendly serving-man, induces the word examples of hypocrisy and deceit. This daemon, it is said, was the constant attendant of Judas Iscariot. The 7th is *Barman*, ready to enter into league with any conjurer, witch, or wizard; but who most commonly possesses the soul of whomsoever he is in league with. These good and evil spirits, it seems, are the most easy to be invoked or called up, agreeably to the desires and situation of the magician's mind and inclination, because they are most near and familiar to the actions and pursuits of men, and officially attendant upon them.

Different from every species of all the foregoing orders of spirits, are the ghosts and apparitions of deceased persons, which have been known for many years to survive and continue; particularly where the deceased person hath departed this life in discontent, melancholy, or unquiet mind; for in these cases they have been often known to return again, and, without a desire of causing terror and alarm to houses and families, seek only for an opportunity of disburthening themselves, that at length they may come into their desired rest. Such persons as are secretly murdered, or that secretly murder themselves, are most apt to appear again, wandering near the place where the catastrophe happened, till the radical moisture of the body be totally consumed. After which, according to the opinion of Paracelsus, and many other learned writers, they can appear no more, but are resolved into their first being or *astum*, after a certain term of years, when the *humidum radicale* becomes exsiccate and dried up, according to the vigour or force of that first attraction, which was the only cause of their returning. And hence was derived the custom of urns and funeral piles amongst the Romans, who used to reduce the corpses of their deceased friends to ashes, lest their ghosts should return and wander; which it was supposed they could not do when the body was burnt, and all moisture totally exterminated and consumed thereby.

The manner and seasons wherein apparitions, and ghosts appear are as various as they are uncertain. Sometimes, before the person to whom they properly belong departs this life, they will, by external, visible presentation of themselves, forewarn him of the time or day wherein death shall approach him. Sometimes the apparition of a person will appear to its beloved friend, husband, wife, or relation, at many thousand miles distance, to acquaint them of its departure from this life whilst otherwise the party would be totally ignorant of this event. And it has often been known, that when no one individual of the kindred or family of the deceased person has been visited or disturbed by it, or even made sensible of its appearing, yet to some of its most intimate or beloved acquaintance it discovers itself, and importunes them to perform some ceremony or promise, that it may be admitted into rest. At other times it discovers some treasure which was hidden by the deceased party; or else some murder which it had committed. But the most frequent cause of their returning is when the party himself hath been privately murdered; for such is the poisonous malice and rancorous spirit of murderers, that innocent blood, thus inhumanly spilt, crieth up to heaven, and the departed spirit cannot rest till the murder be made manifest to the world, after which discovery it is received into rest. This is the reason why, for many years together, ghosts continue to be seen in one particular place, ever watching for fit opportunity to discover or make known the cause of their appearing; but which is often attended with great difficulty and delay, as well on account of the natural timidity of human beings, as for want of the proper organs of corporeal voice and touch in the spirit, which, being no part of their quality or essence, is procured with great difficulty, and at best but inarticulate, doleful, and in broken accents. That this is true, the usual manner, of their appearance in a great measure proves; for all that they are able to effect, if they have been murdered, is to appear near the place where the body lies, and to seem as if they sunk down or vanished in the same; or else to appear in the form of a murdered corpse, with mangled body and bleeding wounds, dishevelled hair and convulsive countenance; but it is rarely known that such apparitions have plainly spoken, or uttered, by words, either the time and place of their murder, or the cause, manner or person's name; unless the perpetration of the deed be marked with circumstances uncommonly horrid and execrable in which cases, I am told, the remembrance of the same doth so much more powerfully operate upon the faculties of the apparition as to enable it to frame the similitude of a voice, so as to discover the fact, and give some leading clue to detect and punish the wicked perpetrator.

But, to give a reason why apparitions are so seldom seen, and why those which do appear cannot without man's assistance accomplish their design, it may easily be conceived, that all spirits, or spiritual substances, of what denomination soever, have their life, breath, and vital motion, in another source, very different from the elements of this external world; and consequently that their manifestation and continuance in this source, whenever they appear, must be both painful and irksome; as it would be for a man to continue with his head under, water, or for the inhabitants of the watery element to be placed upon dry land. But it is only the apparitions of persons thus suddenly taken off in their sins, or of such as die in confirmed and habitual wickedness, that, in the natural course of things, are subject to return into the terrestrial source, and manifest themselves to human eyes. For those who die in perfect peace, with minds divested by true repentance of every turbulent and sinful desire, enter at once into, their desired rest, without the possibility of returning to this sublunary world again, but in the capacity of angels of light, to execute the divine missions of the Deity.

In the writings of Plato, there are many strange and singular representations of the apparitions or departed souls of men, with accounts of their torments and purgations, the cause of their returning, what their nature and employment are, their substance and property, food and nourishment; from all which that great philosopher and historian was induced to believe, that, when the spirits of good and exemplary men returned, it was to persons of a like habit and disposition with themselves, warning them in their sleep of certain dangers or malevolent designs forming against them; or else conveying heavenly doctrines or ingenious inventions to their mind, for the honour of religion or the good of society. And in like manner, if the ghost of a wicked and execrable character returned, it was to those of a profligate and abandoned course of life, whom it instigates, asleep or awake, to the invention and exercise of notorious villainies, to blasphemies against God, and to sedition, rapine, and murder, amongst men. The disciples of Pythagoras established an opinion not very different from this. They held that there was a continual traduction and transmigration of souls from one state to another, till they became deified at last: and that they frequently appeared to persons of the same bent of mind and inclination, to instruct and forewarn them. It was also the opinion of many great and wise philosophers, that the Oracles of old proceeded from such spirits as had been the ghosts of departed souls of wise and excellent men; as the oracle of Apollo, the oracle of Pallas, or Minerva, and the like. And, upon the whole, the variety of examples throughout the writings of wise and learned men, in all ages of the world, in all countries, and in the sacred as well as the profane history, of the various appearances of ghosts and apparitions of departed men, as well as of spirits of other kinds and properties, afford a stronger inducement to our belief of their existence and agency in this sublunary world, than we should, in this more learned and enlightened age, be otherwise willing to admit as an article of our belief. But, seeing these things *are absolutely so,* we will now give some particulars of the mode and manner in which magicians and other professors of the Black

Art obtain an intercourse with them; from which it will appear, that the Science of Astrology is an art founded on philosophy and mathematical demonstration, and totally unconnected with any agency but what proceeds from second causes under God and Nature; whereas the other is a wicked confederation with evil spirits, which ought to be discouraged and suppressed by the utmost exertions of the iron arm of the law.

To the honour of the present century, we have had but few instances of persons openly and publicly entering into compact with spirits, or of professing to resolve questions in futurity by means of their agency; but, prior to that aera, it was no uncommon thing; and those who had an opportunity of blending classical learning and scientific speculation with it were esteemed the most elevated characters of their day, and were frequently honoured with the protection and confidence of princes and other men of rank and fortune. I shall here mention a few of those characters who were esteemed the most considerable magicians of their time.

Apollonius Tyaneus, in the time of the Emperor Domitian, from the wonderful and miraculous things he did through the agency of spirits, added to the great appearance of sanctity and simplicity with which his exterior was endowed by nature, occasioned all ranks of people to regard him with a mixture of reverential awe and respect. Even the Christians, who lived within the circle of his fame, thought him something more than human, and looked up to him with confidence and esteem. From a variety of circumstances, and accounts in different authors, it appears that this singular character had not only the faculty of knowing what was transacting at many hundred miles distance, but had the means also of being conveyed almost instantaneously from one place to another, where he was seen, known, and conversed with many of his acquaintance. It is also recorded of him, that, at the instant the Emperor Domitian was assassinated at Rome, he spoke of it in a public assembly at Ephesus, and declared the mode and manner of his death; which, upon enquiry, was found to happen at the precise moment of time he spoke of it, and in the exact manner he bad described. See p. 40.

Doctor Dee was another very extraordinary character of the same class, and a native of this island. He was not only a famous magician, but a great author, having written upwards of forty-eight different volumes, the first of which was published in 1594. A full account of his convention and intercourse with spirits is now extant, written with his own hand,

and esteemed a very curious and singular performance. His company and acquaintance were much sought by the Emperor Charles V. and by Ferdinand his brother; and, during his travels over the continent, he had not only every respect and attention paid him, but his company was courted by all the learned and religious people wherever he went. He was certainly one of the most learned men of the age in which he lived; and had collected a library of upwards of 4000 volumes of curious and valuable writings, mostly upon physical, theological, and occult, subjects, which he had the misfortune to see burnt by the fury of a mob, who assailed his house, and conspired against his life, under an idea that by magical spells and incantations he had altered the natural course of the weather, and brought on storms, hurricanes, tempests, and continual rain, in order to ruin the harvest; and destroy the fruits of the earth. Yet he bore the torrent and fury of this infatuated multitude with the greatest composure, saying, "They would see their error soon enough to treat him with greater kindness hereafter, than their persecution was now cruel." And so it happened; for, having by means of his confederacy with spirits, foretold and detected a fatal conspiracy against his country, he was then as much honoured and caressed as he had before been stigmatized and abused by the hasty multitude. He wrote the mathematical preface to Euclid's Elements, and has left tables of the harmony and extent of numbers infinitely beyond the capacity of the present times, though so much more learned and refined.

Edward Kelly was also a famous magician, and the companion and associate of Dr. Dee in most of his magical operations and exploits; having been brought in unison with him (as the doctor himself declares, in the preface to his work upon the ministration of spirits) by mediation of the angel Uriel. But Dr. Dee was undoubtedly deceived in his opinion, that the spirits which ministered to him were executing the divine will, and were the messengers and servants of the Deity. Throughout his writings on the subject, he evidently considers them in this light, which is still more indisputably confirmed by the piety and devotion invariably observed at all times when these spirits had intercourse with him. And further, when he found his coadjutor Kelly was degenerating into the lowest and worst species of the magic art, for the purposes of fraud and avaricious gain, he broke off all manner of connexion with him, and would never after be seen in his company. But it is believed, that the doctor, a little before his death, became sensible that he had been imposed upon by these invisible agents, and that all their pretences of acting under the auspices of the angel Uriel, and for the honour and glory of God, were but mere hypocrisy, and the delusions of the devil. Kelly, being thus rejected and discountenanced by the doctor, betook himself to the meanest and most vile practices of the magic-art; in all which pursuits money, and the works of the devil, appear to have been his chief aim. Many wicked and abominable transactions are recorded of him, which were performed by witchcraft, and the mediation of infernal spirits; but nothing more curious, or more *à propos* to the present subject, than what is mentioned by Weaver, in his Funeral Monuments. He there records, that Edward Kelly the magician, with one Paul Waring, who acted in capacity of companion and associate in all his conjurations, went together to the church-yard of Walton Ledale, in the county of Lancaster, where they had information of a person being interred, who was supposed to have hidden or buried a considerable sum of money, and to have died without disclosing to any person where it was deposited. They entered the church-yard exactly at twelve o'clock at night; and having had the grave pointed out to them the preceding day, they exorcised the spirit of the deceased by magical spells and incantations, till it appeared before them, and not only satisfied their wicked desires, and enquiries, but delivered several strange predictions concerning persons in that neighbourhood, which were literally and exactly fulfilled. It was vulgarly reported of Kelly, that he outlived the time of his compact with the devil, and was seized at midnight by some infernal spirits, who carried him off in sight of his own wife and children, at the instant he was meditating a mischievous scheme against the minister of his parish, with whom he was greatly at enmity.

The character of *Mahomet* is too well known throughout all the world, as the institutor of the Turkish Alcoran, to need much comment from me in this place. It is sufficient if I only remark, that all his wonderful miracles were wrought by the aid and confederacy of familiar spirits, which he called the ministration of angels from heaven, from whence he pretended to have been sent, to perform the commands of the Deity, and to correct and reform the manners and religion of mankind. He had the peculiar address to establish this idea amongst his contemporaries, and to lay the foundation of the present faith at Constantinople, and throughout the vast extent of the Turkish territory.

Roger Bacon was another very famous associate with familiar spirits, and performed many astonishing exploits through their means. He was born at Ilchester in Somersetshire, where he studied philosophy, alchymy, and astrology; and wrote several learned and ingenious, books, the manuscripts of which are now preserved as valuable curiosities in the British Museum. I attempted to make some interesting extracts from them, for the further amusement and information of my readers in this part of my work; but I was prevented from going on with my plan, under an idea that the information it would convey might be productive of mischievous consequences to society, by putting too much in the power of evil-minded and vindictive men.

Paracelsus was a great cabalist, physician, astrologer, and magician, and appears to have been intimately acquainted with all the secret and occult properties of nature. He was the first we know of who ever treated upon *animal magnetism;* and his performances in that line were such as to astonish the world, and to draw upon him the united gratulations of the diseased and infirm. His method, notwithstanding it is so clearly laid down by himself, and demonstrated by a variety of pleasing examples in his works, has lain dormant till the present time; and now it begins again, under the successful endeavours of a few persevering individuals to convince mankind that the secret and occult properties of nature are not yet half known or understood; nor their advantages received with that thankfulness and regard which ought incessantly to be poured forth to the great Author of our being, for the blessings that may so easily be derived from them. This was the opinion and nearly the words of Paracelsus himself, who hath been recorded by all our biographers, as a learned, judicious, and ingenious, philosopher. Yet his having been so much addicted to magical rites and ceremonies, and having had familiarity with spirits and devils, and performed so many wonderful conjurations through their means, caused him to have been ever supposed to have done by the agency of spirits what was really the true and genuine effects of nature only.—In the annexed engraving I have given portraits of the above six extraordinary personages.

As to the particular forms, manner, method rites, ceremonies, consecrations, time, place, and ability, requisite to call up and enter into compact or familiarity with spirits, it is neither safe nor prudent, nor consistent with the well-being of society in general, that I should dwell extensively upon it, or give such explanation, as to put a weapon into the hands of the blood-thirsty or revengeful, to despite their enemies or neighbours, or to enable those who are prone to such dealings from idle curiosity, completely to put in execution this species of league with the devil or his subordinate agents; which is as strictly forbidden by the word of God as by the laws of the land. Let it suffice, therefore, what should

Illustration 1

A Type or Figure of a Circle for the Master and his Fellows, to sit in shewing how and after what fashion it should be made

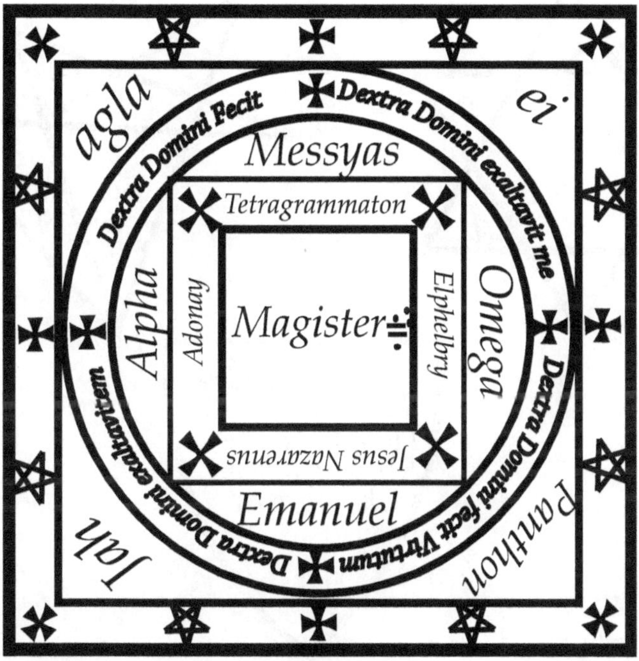

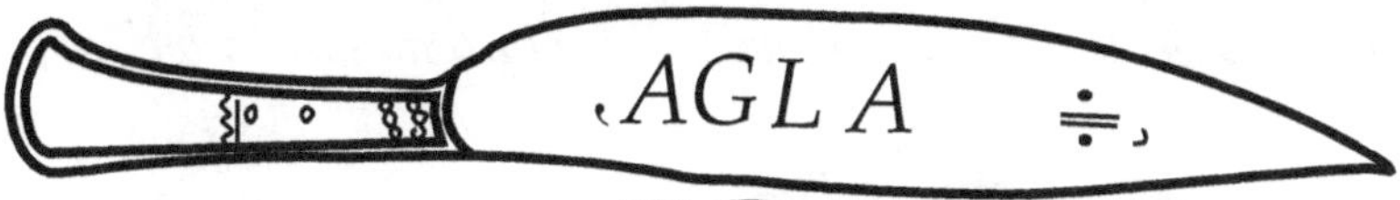

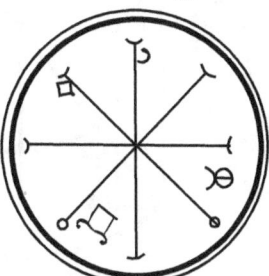

This on the other Side 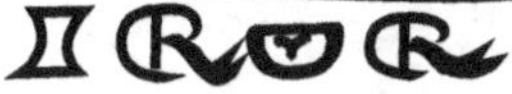

Whosever beareth this sign the spirits will do him homage

Whosever beareth this sign need fear no foe

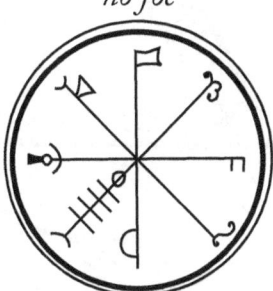

Illustration 2

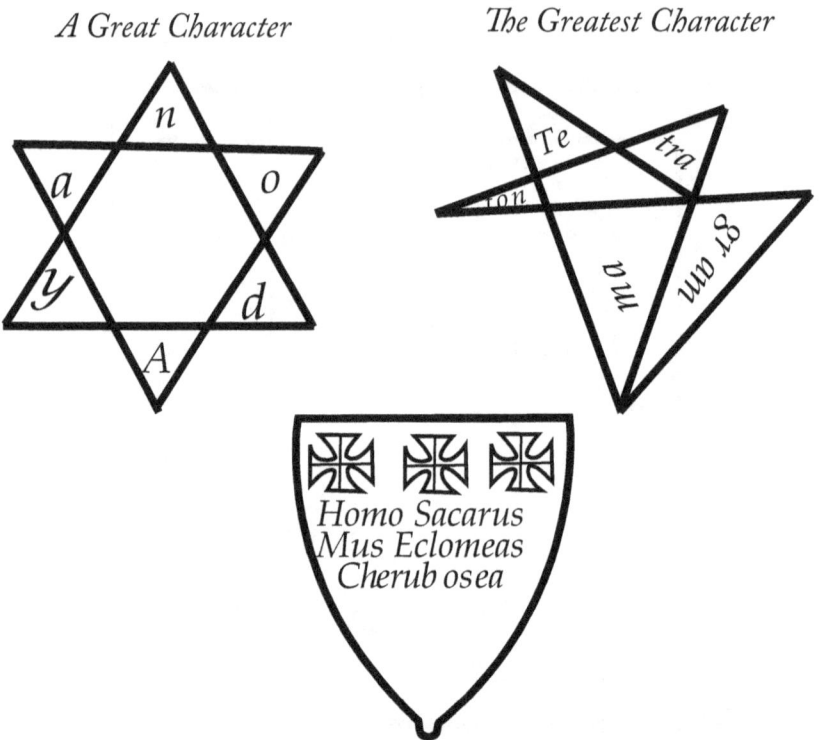

A Great Character

The Greatest Character

The Two Seals of the Earth without which no spirits will appear

give such an outline of it, as may enable the inquisitive reader sufficiently to judge of its merits, without enabling the viciously-inclined to adopt its practice.

Magicians and conjurors who have written upon and followed the Black Art, contend, that it is possible to raise up and hold an intercourse with spirits, and make them subservient to their commands, without any absolute compact or bargain with the devil, either for body, soul, or works; though they are ready to admit, that such a snare is eventually intended for them, by their officiousness upon every occasion, and they are as willing to believe that it has induced many of its practitioners to form such a league. Many instances indeed have been adduced in proof of this, where, at the expiration of a certain term, the devoted wretch has been carried off in the height of his sin and wickedness, by some of the infernal messengers. Such is recorded to have been the case with several in this island; such also was the case with *Lewis Gaufridi*, a French priest, who, to be revenged of some of his superiors for not promoting him to the extent of his ambition, compacted with the devil for fourteen years power, to commit whatever detestable works he pleased without detection or discovery. So likewise, a certain execrable character, who a few centuries back overran this country, was at length publicly taken off in fire and flame, before the eyes of a vast multitude, having covenanted for body, soul, and works. It is to be noted, that, where a compact is formed, the devil, or familiar spirit, is ever at hand, and ready to obey the magician's will, without ceremony or trouble; but where no such league or compact exists, and the magician is desirous of bringing up or *constraining* some particular spirit or ghost to appear before him, there are many rites and ceremonies to be performed, in the first place they are to fix upon a spot proper for such a purpose; which must be either in a subterraneous vault hung round with black, and lighted with a magical torch; or else in the centre of some thick wood or desert, or upon some extensive unfrequented plain, where several roads meet; or amidst the ruins of ancient castles, abbeys, monasteries, &c. or amongst the rocks on the sea-shore; in some private detached church-yard, or any other solemn melancholy place, between the hours of twelve and one in the night, either when the moon shines very bright, or else when the elements are disturbed with storms of thunder, lightning, wind, and rain; for in these places, times, and seasons, it is contended, that spirits can with less difficulty manifest themselves to mortal eyes, and continue visible with the least pain, in this elemental external world.

When the proper time and place are fixed on, a magic circle is to be formed, within which, the master and his associate (for in all these cases there must be two persons) are carefully to retire. The dimensions of the circle are as follow: A piece of ground is generally chosen nine feet square, at the full extent of which parallel lines are drawn one within another, having sundry crosses and triangles described between them, close to which is formed the first or outer circle; then, about half a foot within the same, a second circle is described; and within that another square correspondent with the first, the centre of which is the seat or spot where the master and associate are to be placed. The vacancies formed by the various lines and angles of the figure are filled up with all the holy names of God, having crosses and triangles described between them, agreeable to a sketch I have given in the annexed plate, where likewise I have projected the form of magic seals, pentacles, &c. &c. just to give the reader an idea of what is meant when we have occasion to speak of them in the following discourse. The reasons assigned by magicians and others for the institution and use of circles, is, that so much ground being blessed and consecrated by such holy words and ceremonies as they make use of in forming it, hath a secret force to expel all evil spirits from the bounds thereof; and, being sprinkled with pure sanctified water, the ground is purified from all uncleanness; besides, the holy name of God being written over every part of it, its force becomes so powerful, that no evil spirit hath ability to break through it, or to get at the magician or his companion, by reason of the antipathy in nature they bear to these sacred names. And the reason, they give for the triangles is, that, if the spirit be not easily brought to speak the truth, they may by the Exorcise by conjured to enter the same; where, by virtue of the names of the Essence and Divinity, of God, they can speak nothing but what is true and right. The circle therefore, according to this account of it, is the principal fort and shield of the magician, from which he is not, at the peril of his life, to depart, till he has completely dismissed the spirit, particularly if he be of a fiery or infernal nature. Instances are recorded of many who perished by this means; particularly Chiancungi, the famous Egyptian fortune teller, who in the last century was so famous in England. He undertook, for a wager, to raise up the spirit Bokim; and, having described the circle, he seated his sister Napala by him as his associate. After frequently repeating the forms of exorcism, and calling upon the spirit to appear, and nothing as yet answering his demand, they grew impatient of the business, and quitted the circle, but it cost them their lives; for they were instantaneously seized and crushed to death by that infernal spirit, who happened not to be sufficiently constrained till that moment to manifest himself to human eyes.—The usual form of consecrating the circle, is as follows:

I, who am the servant of the Highest do, by the virtue of his Holy Name Immanuel, sanctify unto myself the circumference of nine feet round about me, ✠✠✠ *from the east,* Glaurah; *from the west,* Garron; *from the north,* Cabon; *from the south,* Berith; *which ground I take for my proper defence from all malignant spirits, that they may have no power over my soul or body nor come beyond these limitations, but answer truly, being summoned, without daring to transgress their bounds.* Worrh-worrah. harcot. Gambalon. ✠✠✠.

The proper attire or *pontifcalibus* of a magician, is an ephod made of fine white linen, over that a priestly robe of black bombazine, reaching to the ground, with the two seals of the earth, drawn correctly upon virgin parchment, and affixed to the breast of his outer vestment. Round his waist is tied a broad consecrated girdle, with the names *Ya, Yay* ✠ *Aiem Aaie,* ✠ *Elibra* ✠ *Elohim* ✠ *Sadai* ✠ *Pah Adonai* ✠ *tuo robore* ✠ *cinctus sum* ✠. Upon his shoes must be written *Tetragrammaton*, with crosses round about; upon his head a high-crown cap of sable silk; and in his hands a holy bible, printed or written in pure Hebrew. When all these things are prepared, the circle drawn, the ground consecrated, and the Exorcist securely placed within the Circle, he proceeds to call up or conjure the spirit by his proper name, under a form somewhat similar to the following:

I exorcise and conjure thee, thou spirit of (here naming the spirit), *by the holy and wonderful names of the Almighty Jehovah, Athanato* ✠ *Aionos* ✠ *Dominus sempiternus* ✠ *Aletheios* ✠ *Sadai* ✠ *Jehovah, Kedsh, El gabor* ✠ *Deus fortissimus* ✠ *Anapheraton, Amorule, Ameron* ✠✠✠ *Panthon* ✠ *Craton* ✠ *Muridon* ✠ *Jah, Jehovah, Elohim pentessaron* ✠✠ *trinus et unus.* ✠✠✠ Θ *I exorcise and conjure, I invocate and command, thee, thou aforesaid spirit, by the power of angels and archangels, cherubim and seraphim, by the mighty Prince Coronzon, by the blood of Abel, by the righteousness of Seth and the prayers of Noah, by the voices of Thunder and dreadful day of Judgment; by all these powerful and royal words abovesaid, that without delay or malicious intent thou do come before me here, at the circumference of this consecrated circle, to answer my proposals and desires, without any maimer of terrible form, either of thyself or attendants; but only obediently, fairly, and with good intent, to present thyself before me, this circle being my defence, through his power who is Almighty, and hath sanctified the name of the Father, Son, and Holy Ghost.* Amen.

After these forms of conjuration, and just before appearances are expected, the infernal spirits make strange and frightful noises, howlings, tremblings, flashes, and most dreadful shrieks and yells, as forerunners of their presently becoming visible. Their first appearance is generally in the form of fierce and terrible lions or tigers, vomiting forth fire, and roaring hideously about the circle; all which time the Exorcist must not suffer any tremor or dismay; for in that case they will gain the ascendency, and the consequences may touch his life. On the contrary, he must summon up a share of resolution, and continue repeating all the forms of constriction and confinement, until they are drawn nearer to the influence of the triangle, when their forms will change to appearances less ferocious and frightful, and become more submissive and tractable. When the forms of conjuration have in this manner been sufficiently repeated, the spirits forsake their bestial shapes, and endow the human form, appearing like naked men of gentle countenance and behaviour. Yet is the magician to be warily on his guard that they deceive him not by such mild gestures; for they are exceedingly fraudulent and deceitful in their dealings with those who constrain them to appear without compact; having nothing in view but to suborn his mind, or accomplish his destruction. But with such as they have entered into agreement with, they are frequent and officious; yet they more or less require certain oblations, which are frequently made to them, such as fumigations, odours, offerings or sacrifices of blood, fire, wine, ointments, incense, fruits, excrements, herbs, gums, minerals, and other ingredients; by which, from a magical cause, they have more influence and authority over the degenerated souls of men, and can insinuate into their inmost source and affection, piercing even through their bones and marrow, till they have so habituated them to their service, that it becomes their daily and sole delight to accomplish every villany and abomination which the malicious and subtle instigations of Satan might purpose to lead them to. So that the Exorcist must be greatly upon his guard; and, when he has completed the exorcism, and made such enquiries as he wished to obtain from the spirit, he must carefully discharge him by some form or ceremony like the following:

Because thou hast diligently answered my demands, and been ready to come at my first call, I do here license thee to depart unto thy proper place, without injury or danger to man or beast; depart, I say, and be ever ready at my call, being duly exorcised and conjured by sacred rites of Magic. I charge thee to withdraw with quiet and peace; and peace be continued betwixt thee and me, in the name of the Father, Son, and Holy Ghost. Amen.

After this ceremony is finished, the spirit will begin to depart, resuming again the shrieks and noises, with flashes of fire, sulphur, and smoke, which the magician is to endure with patience, until it is entirely gone off, and no signs whatever of such a procedure left. Then he may venture to withdraw from the circle, repeating the Lord's Prayer; after which he may take up the various utensils, and, having destroyed all traces of the circle, may return in safety to his proper home.

But if, instead of infernal or familiar spirits, the ghost or apparition of a departed person is to be exorcised, the process is materially different. The person being fixed on, whose apparition is to be brought up, the magician, with his assistant, must repair to the church-yard or tomb where the deceased was buried, exactly at midnight; as the ceremony can only be performed in the night, between the hours of twelve and one. The grave is first to be opened, or an aperture made, by which access may be had to the naked body. The magician having described the circle, and holding a magic wand in his right hand, while his companion or assistant beareth a consecrated torch, he turns himself to all the four winds, and, touching the dead body three times with the magical wand, repeats as follows:

By the virtue of the holy resurrection, and the torments of the damned, I conjure and exorcise thee, spirit of N. *deceased, to answer my liege demands, being obedient unto these sacred ceremonies, on pain of everlasting torment and distress.* Then let him say, *Berald, Beroald, Balbin gab gabor agaba; Arise, arise, I charge and command thee.*

After which forms and ceremonies, the ghost or apparition will become visible, and answer to any questions put to it by the Exorcist. But if it be desired to put interrogatories to the spirit of any corpse that hath hanged, drowned, or otherwise made away with, itself, the conjuration must be performed while the body hangs, or on the spot where it is first found after the suicide hath been committed, and before it is touched or removed by the coroner's jury. The ceremony is as follows: The Exorcist binds upon the top of his wand a bundle of St. John's wort, or *millies perforatum**, with the head of an owl; and having repaired to the spot

---

* [thousand holes]

where the corpse lies, at twelve o'clock at night, he draws the circle, and solemnly repeats the following words:

By the mysteries of the deep, by the flames of Banal, by the power of the East, and the silence of the night, by the holy rites of Hecate, I conjure and exorcise thee, thou distressed spirit, to present thyself here, and reveal unto me the cause of thy calamity, why thou didst offer violence to thy own liege life, where thou art now in being, and where thou wilt hereafter be. He then, gently smiting the carcase nine times with the rod, says, *I conjure thee, thou spirit of this* N. *deceased, to answer my demands that I am to propound unto thee, as thou ever hopest for the rest of the holy ones, and ease of all thy misery; by the blood of Jesu which he shed for thy soul, I conjure and bind thee to utter unto me what I shall ask thee.*

Then, cutting down the carcase from the tree, they lay his head towards the east; and in the space that this following conjuration is repeating, they set a chaffing-dish of fire at his right hand, into which they pour a little wine, some mastic, and gum aromatic, and lastly a vial full of the sweetest oil, having also a pair of bellows, and some unkindled charcoal to make the fire burn bright at the instant of the carcase's rising. The conjuration is thus:

I conjure thee, thou spirit of N. *that thou do immediately enter into thy ancient body again, and answer to my demands, by virtue of the holy resurrection, and by the posture of the body of the Saviour of the world, I charge thee, I conjure thee, I command thee on pain of the torments and wandering of thrice seven years, which I, by the force of sacred magic rites, have power to inflict upon thee; by thy sighs and groans, I conjure thee to utter thy voice; so help thee God and the prayers of the holy church.* Amen.

Which ceremony being thrice repeated, while the fire is burning with mastic and gum aromatic, the body will begin to rise, and at last will stand upright before the Exorcist, answering, with a faint and hollow voice, the questions propounded unto it: Why it destroyed itself, where its dwelling is, what its food and life are, how long it will be ere it enter into rest, and by what means the magician may assist it to come to rest: Also, of the treasures of this world, where they are hid: Moreover, it can answer very punctually of the places where ghosts reside, and how to communicate with them; teaching the nature of astral spirits and hellish beings, so far as its capacity reacheth. All which when the ghost hath fully answered, the magician ought, out of commiseration and reverence to the deceased, to use what means can possibly be used for the procuring rest unto the spirit. To which effect he must dig a grave, and filling the same half full of quick-lime, and a little salt and common sulphur, put the carcase naked into it; which experiment, next to the burning of the body into ashes, is of great force to quiet and end the disturbance of the astral spirit.

But in this, and in all cases where the ghosts or apparitions of deceased persons are raised up and consulted, great caution is to be observed by the magician to keep close within the circle; for if the magician, by the constellation and position of the stars at his nativity, be in the predicament of those who follow the Black Art for iniquitous purposes, and are so distinguished by the positions of their radical figure of birth, it is very dangerous for such men to conjure any spirits without describing the circle after the form already given, and wearing upon their breast, or holding in their hand, the *Pentacle of Solomon*. For the ghosts of men deceased can easily effect sudden death to the magician born under such a conformation of the planets, even whilst in the act of being exorcised; and it is yet more remarkable, that the genethliacal figures of all persons who are naturally addicted to the pursuit of magical incantations and familiarity with spirits, do almost without exception portend sudden death, or an infamous termination of their existence.

Such are the rites, ceremonies, and modes, by which Exorcists and Magicians obtain familiarity with spirits, and carry on a visible and palpable correspondence with the devil. But, besides these means of working wonders, they have others, of an invisible or occult property, as charms, spells, periapts, and the like, which operate both on the body and mind, by the agency of some secret power which the patient can neither feel nor comprehend. They are of various names, forms, and qualities, according to the use for which they are intended. First, Amulets, which are moulded and engraved in the form of money or coin, under certain forms of consecration; and are hung about the neck in certain planetary hours, for the purpose of provoking to love and familiarity with some certain person desired: Secondly, Spells or Charms, consisting of various forms of words, and magical characters, written on virgin parchment, either with human blood, or ink of a particular quality, and consecrated under certain magical forms and ceremonies, to be worn as Periapts to cure diseases, to drive away evil spirits, to preserve from pestilence and infection, to make the party valiant and intrepid, and for a thousand other purposes. Thirdly,

Corselets, which are the ancient Danish charm, being a kind of necklaces composed of thunder-stones, upon which are engraven certain magical characters, which resist all noxious influences, and all danger from thunder and lightning. Pentacles are a fourth sort of appendix, which conjurors and magicians use, being made with five corners, corresponding to the five senses of man, with their virtue and operation inscribed upon the five corners respectively. They are composed of fine linen doubled up, and done with cerecloth between. This figure the magician holds in his hand, lifting it up from the skirt of his garment, to which it is annexed, whenever spirits that are raised become stubborn and rebellious, refusing to conform to the rites and requisitions of exorcism, and offering menacing looks and actions to the magician; but when these Pentacles are held out to the spirits, with the words *Glauron, Amor, Amorula, Beor, Beorka, Beroald, Anepheraton*, inscribed upon them, they become exceedingly tortured and amazed, and are more mild and tractable. There is likewise another fort of charm called *Telesms*, which is used by magicians when they perform any conjuration or exorcism by moon-light in the mountains or valleys; upon which occasions they usually bury them towards the north, east, west, and south, within a hundred yards of the place where the circle is described; for these Telesms have the occult power of preventing any living creature coming near them until the incantation be performed, except the spirit itself whose presence they ardently desire, and are preparing to summon before them.

But to make fiery and infernal spirits more familiar, magicians have classed them into seven distinct orders, answerable to the nature and qualities of the seven planets; under which they respectively make offerings to them of aromatic fumigations, previous to invoking or calling them up; whereby they conceive the information or assistance required from them will be more easily and expeditiously obtained. Thus the fumigations for spirits under Saturn are made of frankincense-tree, pepper-wort roots, storax, and galbanum; by these the spirits Marbas, Corban, Stilkon, Idas, &c. and all of the first order in the astringency, are appeased and provoked, when the fumes are put upon a tripod in the hour of Saturn according to the planetary division. For spirits under Jupiter, they take lignum aloes, ashtree-keys, benjamin, storax, peacocks-feathers, and lapis lazuli, mixing the same with the blood of a stork, a swallow, or a hart; the brains being also added; the fumes are kindled in Jupiter's hour, and in a place appropriate to his nature. They make fumigations unto such spirits of the order of powers as are under Mars, in the planetary division, with aromatic gum, bdellium, euphorbium, loadstone, hellebore white and black, and an addition of sulphur to make them into an amalgama, with man's blood, and the blood of a black cat; which mixtures are said to be so exceeding magical, that, without any other addition, this fumigation is able of itself to make spirits under Mars appear before the Exorcist. To the spirits under Sol, being of the order of thrones, they likewise suffumigate saffron, musk, laurel, cinnamon, ambergrise, cloves, myrrh, and frankincense, musk, and the balsamic tree, mixed up together with the brains of an eagle and the blood of a white cock, being made up like pills, or little balls, and put upon the tripod. The fumigations appropriate to spirits under Venus, are roses, coral, lignum aloes, and spermaceti, made up with sparrows brains, and blood of pigeons. To those under Mercury, they fumigate frankincense, mastic, cinquefoil, incorporated with the brains of a fox, and the blood of a magpye. To spirits under Luna, fumigations are offered of frogs dried, white poppy-seed, bull's eyes, camphire, and frankincense, incorporated with goose's blood, and *fluxus muliebris**. These are the divisions of spirits under the seven planets, with their fumigations; neither can it be denied, but that in many ceremonies of this kind, there is great inherent virtue, according to the doctrine of sympathy and antipathy, whereby every thing is drawn by its like in the idea, whether by words or actions, according to the saying, *In verbis, herbis, & lapididus, latet virtus*†; so that the ceremonies and charms, with other circumstances used by magicians, are-doubtless prevalent to the accomplishment of that work which they undertake; to wit, The calling up and exorcising of infernal spirits by conjurations.

And as by natural reason every magical charm or receipt had its first institution; in like manner have magicians disposed the matter and manner together with the times of their utensils and instruments according to the principles of nature; as, the hour wherein they compote their garments must either be in the hour of Luna, or else of Saturn, in the Moon's in-crease. Their garments they compose of white linen, black cloth, black cat-skins, wolves, bears, or swine's, skins. The linen, because of its abstracted quality for magic, delights not to have any utensils that are put to common uses. The skins of the aforesaid animals are by reason of the Saturnine and magical qualities in the particles of these beasts. Their sewing-thread is of silk, cat's-gut, man's nerves, asses hair, thongs of skins from men, cats, bats, owls, and moles; all which are enjoined from

---

*[menstrual blood]
†[in words, herbs, and stones, lie hidden virtues]

the like magical cause. Their needles are made of hedge-hog prickles, or bones of any of the above-mentioned animals; their writing-pens are of owls or ravens, their ink of man's blood: their ointment is man's fat, blood, usnea, hog's grease, or oil of whales. Their characters are ancient Hebrew or Samaritan: their speech is Hebrew or Latin. Their paper must be of the membranes of infants, which they call virgin parchment, or of the skins of cats, or kids. They compose their fires of sweet wood, oil, or rosin: and their candles of the fat or marrow of men or children: their vessels are earthern, their candlesticks with three feet, of dead mens bones: Their swords are steel, without guards, the points being reversed. These are their materials, which they particularly choose from the magical qualities whereof they are composed. Neither are the peculiar shapes without a natural cause. Their caps are oval, or like pyramids, with lappets on each side, and fur within: their gowns reach to the ground, being furred with white fox-skins; under which they have a linen garment reaching to their knees. Their girdles are three inches broad; and have, according to its use, many caballistical names, with crosses, trines, and circles, inscribed thereon. Their knives are dagger-fashion; and the circles by which they defend themselves are commonly nine feet in breadth, though the eastern magicians allow but seven; for both of which a natural cause is pretended, in the force and sympathy of numbers.

Such spells or charms as are compounded of some *edible* matter, with magical characters engraven upon them, are successfully given for agues, head-achs, epilepsy, fits of the mother, and the like; and it is remarkable that they operate with most effect on those patients who are ignorant of the charm, or its properties. There are also particular magical characters attributed to the planets, whereof *Telesms, Periapts, Amulets,* and *Philtres,* are composed by buryings under ground, writings, bindings, engravings, allegations, &c. which, done in certain astrological hours, are to conquer enemies, cure diseases, remove obstructions, provoke love, and preserve from evil both the body and the soul, which they contend are effected by mediums of this kind, assisted by the force of imagination. But as for philtres, potions, love-cups, and the like, they unquestionably proceed from a natural cause, and ought not to be classed with the occult properties of charms. There are many natural compositions of herbs and minerals, which have a surprising effect in themselves, without the least assistance from superstitious impressions, or the assistance of super-natural agency. For, in the commixture of bodies of a similar nature, there is a two-fold power and virtue; first, when the celestial properties are duly disposed in any natural substance, then under one form divers influences of superior powers are combined; and secondly, when, from artificial mixtures and compositions of natural things combined amongst themselves in a due and harmonical proportion, they agree with the quality and force of the heavens, under certain correspondent constellations. This proceeds from the occult affinity of natural things amongst themselves, by the force and sympathy of which many astonishing effects are produced.

In the writings of Paracelsus we find many surprising examples of the power of sympathy and antipathy, by means of images, telesms, and amulets, compounded of nothing more than natural ingredients. And he particularly describes an infallible method, by the image of any bird or beast, to destroy it, or to effect its death, though at a distance. So like-wise, by the hair, fat, blood, excrements, or excrescences, of any animal, the diseases of that animal might be cured, and its life preserved or destroyed. This is seen in the *armary unguent*, and *sympathetical powder;* and there are multiplied instances and histories, both at home and abroad, of those who have been burnt, hanged, or otherwise punished, for the use of *waxen images*, which they composed is divers postures, under certain constellations, whereby the persons they were made to represent have been severely tormented, or macerated to death. For, according to the torment or punishment the magician, witch, or wizard, may intend to inflict upon the object of their resentment, so they dispose the hour of the constellation, the quality of the compound, and the posture or semblance of the image; for, if they intend to consume and pine away the health and life of any person they are offended with, they mould his image in wax, of such an ominous form and aspect as may conduce to the extent of their design, making several magical characters upon, the sides of the head, describing the character of the planetary hour upon the breast of the image; the name of the persecuted person on its forehead; and the intended effect to be wrought upon him, on its back. If they mean to produce violent pains and tortures in the flesh or sinews; they stick, pins or thorns, in divers places of the arms, legs, or breast, of the image. If to cast them into violent fevers and consumptions, they spend a certain hour every day to warm and turn the image before a doleful and lingering fire, composed of divers exotic gums and magical ingredients, of sweet odours, and roots of particular shrubs, efficient and conducive to their purpose; and, when the whole operation has been performed, and the image is completed, it is astonishing to human comprehension what surprising effects they are capable of producing upon the body they are intended to represent; and the reader can only attain a competent idea of it by reading the accounts of the trials and confessions of many witches and wizards who suffered the law in the 17th and commencement of the 18th century for transactions of this kind; an incredible number of which are not only recorded in the notes and memorandums, of the judges, but attested by a great variety of noblemen, gentlemen, clergy, physicians, apothecaries, and others, who have been, eye-witnesses of these diabolical proceedings; and for which reason I shall on no account mention the most perfect and effectual part of the composition and preparation of these magical images, lest the evil-minded and malicious part of my readers should attempt to work abominable species of revenge upon the persons or property of their unsuspecting neighbours.

Thousands of other strange and uncouth inventions might be here described, according to the exact form in which tradition hath left them; but, for the reason above assigned, the reader must be content with the general outline only. And, as Europeans have the ability of effecting such astonishing things by the medium of images, telesms, periapts; &c. so the Tartars have a facility of producing similar effects by *bottles, wolves-skins, rods, basins, letters* or *missives*, unto certain familiar spirits, who are the agents in their magic rites. As to the old and favourite trick of witches in the last century, that of *tying of the point*, we have reason to hope it has long since died away; for it is a charm which produces so strong an impediment to conjugal embraces, as totally to restrain the act of consummation betwixt married people; and the tying of this knot or ligament, under certain magical ceremonies or incantations, was so notorious, both in practice and effect, throughout England, France, Spain, Italy, and the eastern countries, that laws were enacted by the legislature in each of those kingdoms expressly to prohibit the performance of it, on pain of death. The form and manner of it is in part mentioned in the statutes, though by no means fit to be openly described here. The art of *Transplantation* is also reckoned amongst charms and sygils; and indeed one part of it, viz. the transferring of diseases, is really magical, and was much in practice amongst witches and wizards; and I am confidently informed is now frequently done in the more remote and unpolished parts of this island. The method is, by giving certain baits or preparations to any domestic animal, they remove fevers, agues, coughs, consumptions, asthmas, &c. from any person applying to them for that purpose; or they can transplant or remove them from one person to another, by burying certain images in their ground, or against their houses, with certain ominous inscriptions and Hebrew words; yet, though these things are supposed to be done by magic, still the efforts are derived more from the sympathies and antipathies in nature, than from magical characters and conjurations; for many persons, without knowing any thing of the cause, how or why it is effected, more than the external forms of words or touch, which is most simple, can remove diseases, take off warts and other excrescences, and perform many surprising cures at a distance from the patient, and even without seeing or knowing him; so by a similar property in the sympathy and antipathy of nature, certain leaves, roots, or juices, rubbed upon warts, or carnous substances, or upon the hands, breast, legs, or other diseased part of the body, and buried under ground, remove or cure the same; which experiments take effect according to the mediums, and their consumption and putrefaction in the mother-earth, of which the human source is principally compounded. Nor is it to be wondered that natural things, being fitted to the times and constellations, and compounded of correspondent or sympathetic ingredients, should produce such effects, without supernatural aid, of the agency of spirits. This is perfectly exemplified in that extraordinary preparation, called a magical candle, which being lighted, foretels the death of the party of whose blood it was prepared. It is compounded after the following manner: They take a good quantity of the venal blood luke-warm as it came out of the vein, which, being chemically prepared with spirits of wine and other ingredients, is at last made up into a candle, which, being once kindled, never goes out till the death of the party whose blood it is composed of; for when he is sick, or in danger, it burns dim and troubled; and when he is dead, it is quite extinguished; of which composition a learned philosopher hath written an entire tract; viz. *De Biolychnio*; or, The Lamp of Life.

In the simple operations of nature many wonderful things are wrought, which upon a superficial view appear impossible, or else to be the work of the devil. These certainly ought to be considered in a far different light from magical performances, and should be classed among the surprising phenomena of nature. Thus lamps or torches made of serpents' skins, and compounded of the fat and spirit of vipers, when lighted in a dark room, will bring the similitude of snakes or serpents writhing and twisting upon the walls. So oil compounded of grapes, being put into a lamp and lighted, will make the room appear to be full of grapes, though in reality it is nothing more than the idea or similitude. The same thing is to be done with all the plants and flowers throughout the vegetable system, by means of a chemical analysis, whereby a simple spirit is produced, which will represent the herb or flower from which it is extracted, in full bloom. And as the process is easy, simple, pleasing, and curious, I will here state it in such a manner as might enable any person to put it in practice at pleasure.

Take any whole herb, or flower, with its root, make it very clean, and bruise it in a stone mortar quite small; then put it into a glass vessel hermetically sealed; but be sure the vessel be two parts in three empty. Then place it for putrefaction in a gentle heat in balneo, not more than blood warm, for six months, by which it will be all resolved into water. Take this water, and pour it into a glass retort, and place a receiver thereunto, the joints of which must be well closed; distil it into a sand-heat until there come forth a water and an oil; and in the upper part of the vessel will hang a volatile salt. Separate the oil from the water, and keep it by itself, but with, the water purify the volatile salt by dissolving, filtering, and coagulating. When the salt is thus purified, imbibe with it the said oil, until it is well combined. Then digest them well together for a month in a vessel hermetically sealed; and by this means will be obtained a most subtile essence, which being held over a gentle heat of a candle, the spirit will fly up into the glass where it is confined, and represent the perfect idea or similitude of that vegetable whereof it is the essence: and in this manner will that thin substance, which is like impalpable ashes or salt, send forth from the bottom of the glass the manifest form of whatever herb it is the *menstruum*, in perfect vegetation, growing by little and little, and putting on so fully the form of stalks, leaves, and flowers, in full and perfect appearance, that any one would believe the same to be natural and corporeal; though at the same time it is nothing more than the spiritual idea endued with a spiritual essence. This shadowed figure, as soon as the vessel is taken from the heat or candle, returns to its *caput mortuum*, or ashes, again, and vanishes away like an apparition, becoming a chaos, or confused matter. For more on the medicinal virtues of decoction of salt, or essence of herbs, flowers, roots, or seeds, see my new edition of CULPEPER'S COMPLETE HERBAL, just published, with Notes, Additions, and Illustrations, in quarto, with upwards of 400 elegant engravings of British Herbs, Plants, and Flowers, coloured to Nature.

To make a vegetable more quickly yield its spirit, take of what vegetable you please, whether it be the seed, flower, root, fruit, or leaves; cut or bruise them small, put them into warm water, put upon them yeast or barm, and cover them up warm, and let them work three days, in the same manner as beer; then distil them, and they will yield their spirit very easily. Or else take of what herbs, flowers, seeds, &c. you please, fill the head of a still therewith, then cover the mouth with coarse canvas, and set on the still, having first put into it a proportionable quantity of sack or low wine; then give it fire, and it will quickly yield its spirit; but observe, that, if the colour of the vegetable is wanted, you must take some of its dried flowers, and fill the nose of the still therewith, and you will have the exact colour of the herb.

To elucidate this process with better effect, I have subjoined a Plate of the Elaboratory, where a person is in the act of producing these flowery apparitions; in which fig. 1 represents a stone pestle and mortar, wherein the herbs, &c. are to be bruised before they are placed for putrefaction. Fig. 2, 2, are glass vessels hermetically sealed, containing the bruised herbs for putrefaction. Fig. 3, an empty glass retort. Fig. 4, a retort filled with the essence of an herb, and put into a sand-heat for distillation. Fig. 5, a glass receiver joined to the retort, to receive the oil and spirit. Fig. 6, a stool on which rests the receiver. Fig. 7, the furnace, made with different conveniences, either for sand-heat, or balnea. Fig. 8, 8, the furnace-holes wherein the fire is placed; Fig. 9, a table whereon are placed the glass vessels hermetically sealed. Fig. 10, a vessel containing the representation or similitude of a pink in full bloom. Fig. 11 is, the representation of sprig of rosemary. Fig. 12, the representation of a sprig of baum. Fig. 13, a candlestick with a candle lighted for the purpose of heating the spirit; Fig. 14, a chemist in the act of holding the glass vessel over the lighted candle; whereby fig. 15 represents the idea of a rose in full bloom.

Now this effect, though very surprising, will not appear so much a subject of our astonishment, if we do but consider the wonderful power of sympathy, which exists throughout the whole system of nature, where every thing is excited to beget or love its like, and is drawn after it, as the loadstone draws iron; the male after the female; the evil after the evil; the good after the good; which is also seen in wicked men and their pursuits, and in birds and beasts of prey; where the lamb delights not with the lion nor the sheep in the society of the wolf; neither do men whose minds are totally depraved and estranged from God care to adopt the opposite qualities, which are virtuous, innocent, and just. Without contemplating these principles, we should think it incredible that the grunting or squeaking of a little pig, or the sight of a simple sheep, should terrify a mighty elephant! and yet by that means the Romans put to flight Pyrrhus and all his host. One would hardly suppose that the crowing of a cock, or the sight of his comb, should abash a puissant lion; but experience has proved the truth of it to all the world. Who would imagine that a poisonous serpent could not live under the shade of an ash-tree; or that some men, deficient neither in courage, strength, or constitution, should not be able to endure the sight of a cat? and yet these things are seen and known to be so, by frequent observation and experience. The friendly intercourse betwixt a fox and a serpent is almost incredible; and how fond and loving the lizard is to man we read in every treatise on natural history; which is not far, if anything, behind the fidelity of a spaniel, and many other species of dogs, whose sagacity and attention to their master is celebrated in an infinite variety of well-founded though almost-incredible stories. The amity betwixt a castrel and a pigeon is remarked by many authors, particularly how curiously the castrel will defend a pigeon from the sparrow-hawks, and other inimical birds. In the vegetable system, the operation and virtue of herbs is at once a subject of admiration and gratitude; and when it were almost endless to repeat* There is among them such natural accord and discord, that some will prosper more luxuriantly in another's company; while some again will droop and die away, being planted near each other. The lily arid the rose rejoice by each other's side; whilst the flag and the fern abhor one another, and will not live together. The cucumber loveth water, but hateth oil; and fruits will neither ripen nor grow in aspects that are inimical to them. In stones likewise, in minerals, and in earth or mould, the same sympathies and antipathies are preserved. Animated nature, in every clime, in every corner of the globe, is also pregnant with similar qualities; and that in a most wonderful and admirable degree. Thus we find that one particular bone taken out of a carp's head will stop an hemorrhage of blood, when no other part or thing in the same creature hath any similar effect. The bone also in a hare's foot instantly mitigates the most excruciating tortures of the cramp; yet no other other bone nor part of that animal can do the like. I might also recite infinite properties with which it has pleased God to endue the form and body of man, which are no less worthy of admiration, and fit for this place, had we but limits to recount them. Indeed I do not know a much more remarkable thing, (were it as rare as it is now shamefully

---

*For the wonderful virtues and properties of herbs and plants, with their alimentary and medicinal qualities; and how to prevent or cure all diseases incident to the human body, at the least expense and at the greatest certainty, see also my new edition of CULPEPER's BRITISH HERBAL, and DOMESTIC PHYSICIAN, printed uniformly with this work, in 2 vols. 4to.

prevalent,) of that would more puzzle our senses, than the effects of intoxication, by which we see a man so totally overthrown, that not a single part or member of his body can perform its function or office; and his understanding, memory, and judgment, so arrested or depraved, that in every thing except the shape, he becomes a very beast! But we find, from observations however important, however wonderful, how inexplicable or miraculous, soever any thing may be, yet if it is common, or familiar to our senses, the wonder ceases, and our enquiries end. And hence it is, that we look not with half the admiration upon the sun, moon, and stars, that we do upon the mechanism of a globe, which does but counterfeit their order, and is a mere bauble, the work of men's hands! whence I might almost be justified in remarking, that, if Christ himself had continued long in the habit of working miracles, and had left that power permanent and hereditary in the Church, they would have long since grown into contempt, and not have been regarded as events worthy of our attention.

From what has been premised, we may readily conclude that there are two distinct species of Magic; one whereof being inherent in the occult properties of Nature, is called *Natural Magic*; and the other, being obnoxious and contrary to Nature, is termed *Infernal Magic*, because it is accomplished by infernal agency or compact with the Devil. Each of these we will consider separately, with the good and evil consequences likely to result from them.

Under the veil of Natural Magic, it hath pleased the Almighty to conceal many valuable and excellent gifts, which common people either think miraculous or next to impossible. And yet in truth, natural magic is nothing more than the workmanship of nature, made manifest by art; for in tillage, as nature produceth corn and herbs, so art, being nature's handmaid, prepareth and helpeth it forward; in which times and seasons are materially to be considered; for *annus, non arvus, producit aristas**. And, though these things, while they lie hid in nature, do many of them seem impossible and miraculous, yet, when they are known and their simplicity revealed, our difficulty of apprehension ceases, and the wonder is at an end; for that only is wonderful to the beholder whereof he can conceive no cause nor reason, according to the saying of Ephesius, *Miraculum solvitur unde videtur esse miraculum*†; yet we often see persons take great pains, and put themselves to vast expence, to discover these impalpable tracks of nature, from whence pecuniary advantages seldom result; so that

*   [a year, not cultivated, produces grain]
†   [the wonder is dissolved from where the wonder is seen]

a man must not learn philosophy to grow rich; but must get riches to learn philosophy. There is unquestionably much praise due, and great industry required, for obtaining a competent knowledge of natural magic; for to sluggards, niggards, and narrow-minded men, the secrets of nature are never opened, though the study of them is certainly conducive to the glory of God, and to the good of society, by more visibly manifesting the omnipotency of his works, and by skilfully applying them to man's use and benefit. Many philosophers of the first eminence, as Plato, Pythagoras, Empedocles, Democritus, &c. travelled through every region of the known world for the accomplishment of this kind of knowledge; and at their return, they publicly preached and taught it. But, above all, we learn from sacred and profane history, that Solomon was the greatest proficient in this art of any either before or since his time; as he himself hath declared in Ecclesiastes and the book of Wisdom, where he saith, "God hath given me the true science of things, so as to know how the world was made, and the power of the elements, the beginning, and the end, and the midst of times, the change of seasons, the courses of the year, and the situation of the stars, the nature of human beings, and the quality of beasts, the power of winds, and the imaginations of the mind; the diversities of plants, the virtues of roots, and all things whatsoever, whether secret or known, manifest or invisible." And hence it was that the magi, or followers of natural magic, were accounted wise, and the study honourable; because it consists in nothing more than the most profound and perfect part of natural philosophy, which defines the nature, causes, and effects, of things.

How far such inventions as are called charms, amulets, periapts, and the like, have any foundation in natural magic, may be worth our enquiry; because, if cures are to be effected through their medium, and that without any thing derogatory to the attributes of the Deity, or the principles of religion, I see no reason why they should be rejected with that inexorable contempt, which levels the works of God with the folly and weakness of men. Not that I would encourage superstition, or become an advocate for a farrago of absurdities; but when the simplicity of natural things, and their effects, are rejected merely to encourage professional artifice and emolument, it is prudent for us to distinguish between the extremes of bigotted superstition and total unbelief.

It was the opinion of many eminent physicians, of the first ability and learning, that such kind of charms or periapts as consisted of certain odoriferous herbs, balsamic roots, mineral concretions, and metallic substances, might have, and most probably possessed, by means of their strong medicinal properties, the virtue of curing or removing such complaints as external applications might effect, and which are often used with success, though without the least surprise or admiration; because the one appears in a great measure to be the consequence of manual operation, which is *perceptible* and *visible* to the senses, whilst the other acts by an innate or occult power, which the eye cannot see, nor the mind so readily comprehend; yet, in both cases, perhaps, the effect is produced by a similar cause; and consequently all such remedies, let them be applied under what form or style they may, are worthy of our regard, and ought to excite in us not only a veneration for the simple practice of the ancients in their medical experiments, but a due sense of gratitude to the wise Author of our being, who enables us, by such easy means, to remove the infirmities incident to mankind. Many reputable authors, particularly A. Ferrarius, Alexander Trallianus, Aetius, Octavianus, Marcellus, Philodotus, Archigines, Philostratus, Pliny, and Dioscorides, contend that not only such physical alligations, appensions, periapts, amulets, charms, &c. which from their materials appear to imbibe and to diffuse the medical properties above described, ought in certain obstinate and equivocal disorders to be applied; but those likewise, which from their external form and composition have no such inherent virtues to recommend them; for harm they can do none, and good they might do; either by accident, or through the force of imagination. And it is asserted, with very great truth, that through the medium of hope and fear, sufficiently impressed upon the mind or imagination, whether by charms, or any other *homerical* contrivance or device, the most wonderful and instantaneous cures are sometimes wrought. They are called homerical devices, or *homerica medicatio*, because Homer was the first who discovered the blood to be suppressed, or its motion accelerated, by the force of imagination; and that diseases were to be removed or terminated thereby. Of the truth of this we have the strongest and most infallible evidence in the hiccough, which is instantaneously cured by any sudden effect of fear or surprise; so likewise agues and many other maladies are removed; and to the same cause we might attribute the only *certain* cure known for the bite of a mad dog, which is the effect of fear and stagnation wrought upon the mass of blood by immerging the body in the sea. Nor are the instances few, where persons lying bed-ridden, and unable to move either hand or foot, have, through the sudden fright of fire, or the house falling in upon them, forgot their infirmity, and run away with as much activity as though no such malady had existed. Seeing, therefore, that such virtues lie hid in the occult properties of nature, united with the sense or imagination of man, where one is the agent, and the other the patient; where the one is active, and the other passive, without any compact with spirits, or dealings with the devil; we surely ought to receive them into our practice, and to adopt them as often as occasion seriously requires, although professional emolument, and pecuniary advantage, might in some instances be narrowed by it.

But, though I might be an advocate for such charms or occult remedies as are in themselves perfectly innocent and simple, I by no means wish it to be understood, that I either approve or recommend any thing bordering upon such inventions as are obviously founded in magical confederacy, and act by the medium of aerial or infernal spirits. To that mind, which has but slightly contemplated the works of nature, it must be abundantly evident, that the great and good God which sustains and governs the universe, hath in the works of creation mercifully afforded us a natural remedy for all our infirmities; and it is repugnant to common sense, and incompatible with religion and morality; nay, it would imply a deficiency either in the goodness or power of the Deity, were we for a moment to admit the necessity of charms, amulets, or any other inventive cures or benefits to men, resulting from a compact with spirits, in which all the powers and performances of witchcraft had their beginning; and therefore we may without the smallest hesitation conclude, that whatever hath its foundation in such confederacy, let the external object or pretence be what it may, it is not only contrary to nature, but highly offensive to the Deity; and nearly allied to the shocking sin of idolatry, by applying the works of God to the power of the devil. For this reason, it is impossible to be too cautious how the use of such descriptions of charms or lamins is adopted, where, instead of natural medicaments, magical characters, incantations, and nocturnal ceremonies, constitute the component parts. A very wise and learned author, who has written largely upon this subject, asserts, that in those very charms and signatures compacts themselves are virtually contained, which evil spirits at first subtilly devised or invented to blind men's eyes, that thereby they might lead them less scrupulously into the snares of the devil. And hence we have good ground to believe, that none are able absolutely, and bona fide, to call up any spirits, without some such compact first formed; and that whosoever has so far ventured in the art of magic or conjuration, hath, though to himself perhaps unknown, compared with and worshipped the devil, under some such form of mystical words and characters wherewith infernal charms and amulets are composed; neither is it to be thought a matter of surprise, that such a compact should unwittingly be made through the medium of those mystical characters, which, with the devil's aid, have in themselves a power to enchant, infect, allure, preserve, or destroy. And to show, in striking colours, the danger of being drawn away by such allurements, I shall instance the extraordinary case of a very harmless and well-meaning young man, which was published to the world at the commencement of the present century, by the Bishop of Gloucester, in the following well-authenticated letter to that prelate.

AUTHENTIC COPY *of a* LETTER *sent to the Bishop of Gloucester, by the Reverend Mr. Arthur Bedford, Minister of Temple Church, in Bristol.*

MY LORD,   *Bristol, August* 2, 1703.

Being informed by Mr. Shute of your lordship's desire that I should communicate to you what I had known concerning a certain person, who was acquainted with spirits to his own destruction, I have made bold to give you the trouble of this letter, hoping my desire to gratify your lordship in every particular may be an apology for the length thereof. I had formerly given an account to the late Bishop of Hereford, in which there are probably some things contained, which I do not now remember, which, if your lordship could procure from his lady, (who now lives near Gloucester,) would be more authentic.

About thirteen years ago, whilst I was curate to Dr. Read, rector of St. Nicholas in this city, I began to be acquainted with one Thomas Perks, a man about twenty years of age, who lived with his father at Mongatsfield, a gunsmith; and contracted an intimacy with him, he being not only a very good-natured man, but extremely skilled in mathematical studies, which were his constant delight, viz. arithmetic, geometry, gauging, surveying, astronomy, and algebra; he had a notion of the perpetual motion, much like that wheel in Archimedes's Mathematical Magic, in which he had made some improvements, and which he has held was demonstrable from mathematical principles, though I could never believe it. I have seen an iron wheel, to which he intended to add several things of his own invention, in order to finish the same; but, thinking it of no use, and being otherwise unfortunately engaged, it was never perfected. He gave himself so much to astronomy, that he could not only calculate the motions of the planets, but an eclipse also, and demonstrate any problem in spherical trigonometry from mathematical principles, in which he discovered a clear force of reason. When one Mr. Bailey, minister of St. James's in this city, endeavoured to set up a mathematical school, I advised him to this Thomas Perks, for an acquaintance, in whom, as he told me, he found a greater proficiency in those studies than he expected or could have imagined. After this he applied himself to astrology, and would sometimes calculate nativities and resolve horary questions. When by the providence of God I was settled in Temple-parish, and had not seen him for some time, he came to me, and, we being in private, he asked my opinion very seriously concerning the lawfulness of conversing with spirits; and, after I had given my thoughts in the negative, and confirmed them with the best reason I could, he told me he had considered all these arguments, and believed they only related to conjurations, but there was an innocent society with them which a man might use, if he made no compact with them, did no harm by their means, and were not curious in prying into hidden things; and that he himself had discoursed with them, and heard them sing to his great satisfaction; and gave an offer to me and Mr. Bayley at another time, that, if we would go with him one night to Kingswood, we should see them, and hear them both talk and sing, and talk with them whenever we had a mind, and we should return very safe; but neither of us had the courage to venture. I told him the subtilty of the devil to delude mankind, and to transform himself into an angel of light; but he would not believe it was the devil. I had several conferences with him upon this subject, but could never convince him, in all which I could never observe the least disorder of mind, his discourse being very rational; and I proposed (to try him) a question in astronomy relating to the projection of the sphere, which he projected and resolved, and did afterwards demonstrate from the mathematics, so as to show at the same time that his brain was free from the least tincture of madness and distraction.— Having this opportunity of asking him several particulars, concerning the methods he used, and the discourses he had with them, he told me he had a book whose directions he followed, and accordingly, in the dead time of the night, he went out to a cross way, with a lanthorn and candle consecrated for this purpose with several incantations. He had also consecrated chalk, consisting of several mixtures, with which he made a circle at what distance he thought fit, within which no spirit had power to enter. After this he invoked the spirit by several forms of words, (some of which he told me were taken out of the holy Scriptures, and therefore he thought them lawful, without considering how they might be wrested to his destruction;) accordingly the spirits appeared to him which he called for, in the shape of little maidens, about a foot and half high, and played about a circle. At first he was some-what affrighted; but, after some small acquaintance, this antipathy in nature wore off, and he became pleased with their company. He told me they spoke with a very shrill voice, like an ancient woman. He asked them if there was a heaven or hell ? they said there was. He asked them what place heaven was ? which they described as a place of great glory and happiness; and he asked them what hell was ? and they bade him ask no questions of that nature, for it was a dreadful thing to relate, and the devils believe and tremble. He further asked them what method or order they had among themselves ? they told him they were divided into three orders; that they had a chief whose residence was in the air; that he had several counsellors which were placed by him in form of globe, and he in the centre, which was the chiefest order; another order was employed in going to and from thence to the earth, to carry intelligence from those lower Spirits; and their own order was on the earth, according to the directions they should receive from those in the air.

This description was very surprising, but, being contrary to the account we have in Scripture of the hierarchy of the blessed angels, made me conclude they were devils, but I could not convince him of it. He told me he had bade them sing, and they went to some distance behind a bush, from whence he could hear a perfect concert of such exquisite music as he never before heard; and in the upper part he heard something very harsh and shrill like a reed, but, as it was managed, did give a particular grace to the rest.

About a quarter of a year after he came again to me, and wished he had taken my advice, for he thought, he had done that which would cost him his life, and which he did heartily repent of; and indeed his eyes and countenance showed a great alteration. I asked him what he had done. He told me that, being bewitched to his acquaintance, he resolved to proceed farther in this art, and to have some familiar spirit at his command, according to the directions of his book, which were as follows:-

He was to have a book made of virgin parchment consecrated with several incantations; likewise a particular ink-horn, ink, &c. for his purpose; with these he was to go out as usual to a cross way, and call up a spirit, and ask him his name, which he was to put in the first page of his book, and this was to be his familiar. Thus he was to do by as many as he pleased, writing their names in distinct pages, only one in a leaf; and then, whenever he took the book and opened it, the spirit whose name appeared should appear also; and, putting this in practice, the familiar he had was called Malchi, a word in Hebrew of an unknown signification. After this they appeared faster than he desired, and in most dismal shapes, like serpents, lions, bears, &c. hissing at him, and attempting to throw spears and balls of fire, which did very much affright him, and the more when he found it not in his power to stay them, insomuch that his hair (as he told me) stood upright, and he expected every moment to be torn in pieces; this happened in December about midnight, when he continued there in a sweat till break of day, and then they left him, and from that time he was never well as long as he lived. In his sickness he came frequently to Bristol, to consult with Mr. Jacob, an apothecary in Broad-street, concerning a cure, but I know not whether he told him the origin of his sickness or not; he also came to me at the same time, and owned every matter of fact until the last, and insisted that, when he did any thing of this nature, he was deluded in his conscience to think it lawful, but he was since convinced to the contrary. He declared he made no compacts with any of those spirits, and never did any harm by their means, nor ever pryed into the future fortune of himself or others, and expressed a hearty repentance and detestation of his sins; so that, though those methods cost him his life in this world, yet I have great reason to believe him happy in the other. I am not certain that he gave this account to any other person but myself, though he communicated something of it to Mr. Bayley, minister of St. James's, in this city; perhaps your lordship may be further informed by his relations and neighbours of Mangotsfield, which lies in Gloucestershire, not above a mile out of the road to Bath.

I have frequently told this story, but never mentioned his name before, and therefore, if your lordship hath any design of printing such accounts as these, I desire it may be with such tenderness to his memory as he deserved, and so as may not be the least prejudice to his relations, who have the deserved character of honest and sober people. I am

Your Lordship's dutiful

Son and Servant,

ARTHUR BEDFORD,

This poor deluded young man, it is very apparent, had no evil design, but entered into this infernal association for no other motive than to gratify an idle curiosity; the consequence of which was that he underwent the most indescribable terror and fright, which at first deprived him of his health, and eventually of his life. I have no doubt but the circumstance of *disbelieving the existence of spirits* (which I apprehend is more or less the case with most people) was the first, if not the only, inducement that urged him to make the experiment. There are many instances of a similar kind, equally well founded, and as fatal in their consequences, which might be here adduced, to show the dreadful effects of being led away by a presumptuous or a hardened mind, to disbelieve the word of God revealed in a thousand passages of scripture, where this infernal intercourse is seriously forbidden; but I sincerely hope, and have reason to believe, that this example will operate as a sufficient bar against all similar enquiries, where it is once read, and the melancholy consequences duly considered. Wherefore let me entreat all my readers to stifle every inordinate desire, which might unguardedly prompt them to solicit an intercourse with such dangerous company; not to attempt the conjuration of spirits of any description or order; no, not even out of joke or bravado, or for fun or frolic; for the devils are continually going about "*seeking whom they may devour;*" they are ever on the watch, and ready at hand to catch at every thought that might be turned to their purpose; and, when they have once so far succeeded as to occupy the smallest place in the mind, I fear it will prove no easy task to dispossess them.

Let it ever be remembered, that the first assaults of wicked spirits are usually made upon our sensual desires, whereby they insinuate themselves into our very appetites, enticing our inclinations, and depraving the moral faculties of the mind; until they become, as it were, incorporated with our nature, leading us insensibly from folly to vice, until a depravity of heart and an obstinate will betray us into a corporal as well as spiritual compact with the devil. These considerations, seconded by an anxious wish to rescue the astral science from the imputation of magical and diabolical connection, and which, I trust, I have fully and effectually accomplished, were the grand inducements that led me to explore the spiritual and infernal kingdoms, and to expose the iniquity, as well as to explain the theory, of familiarity or compact with them. And in doing this, I have scrupulously avoided giving the essential forms and particular consecrations adapted to mystical performances, lest the unwary speculator might carry his experiments too far, and, as in the example before us, unwittingly seek his own destruction. Yet I have, as far as safety or conveniency would permit, explained the speculative part; reserving only those special forms and incantations, which, being not only very facile but of wonderful occult power, would be dangerous to disclose; and at best could only serve to strengthen the hands of the malicious and evil-minded, or to extend more widely the infernal empire; against which we ought to put on *the whole armour of God; for we wrestle not against flesh and blood, but against principalities and powers; for which cause we should resolutely withstand the assaults of the devil, our loins being girt about with verity, and having on the breast-plate of righteousness.* Nor let us vainly seek to know the mysteries of the other world, farther than it hath pleased God to reveal them to us by his divine word; for, *infiniti ad finitum nulla est proportio, necque loci potest circumscribi;* " of that which is finite to that which is infinite, there is no proportion; neither can that which is immeasurable be contained within the limits of space, or be defined by human comprehension!"

www.ingramcontent.com/pod-product-compliance
Lightning Source LLC
Chambersburg PA
CBHW020803160426
43192CB00006B/420